SPENSER'S
FAERIE QUEENE

To
ELEANOR C. LODGE
in grateful Friendship

SPENSER'S FAERIE QUEENE

An Interpretation

By

JANET SPENS, M.A., D.Litt.

FELLOW AND TUTOR OF LADY MARGARET HALL, OXFORD

NEW YORK / RUSSELL & RUSSELL

FIRST PUBLISHED IN 1934
REISSUED, 1967, BY RUSSELL & RUSSELL
A DIVISION OF ATHENEUM PUBLISHERS, INC.
BY ARRANGEMENT WITH THE ESTATE OF JANET SPENS
L. C. CATALOG CARD NO: 66-27149
PRINTED IN THE UNITED STATES OF AMERICA

Preface

Short as it is, this book has been on the stocks for more than five years. During that time the river of American critical work on Spenser, already a considerable stream, has risen to a flood. Two courses were open to me: either to make a complete study of this critical work, and answer or incorporate its conclusions in my own book; or to ignore it, only taking cognizance of it where its results seemed certain, and would invalidate my own theories. I chose the second course, and have tried to read all books and articles, the titles or available synopses of which suggested that they would cut across my ground. On the whole it has not seemed necessary to deal directly with them. Much useful and stimulating work, for example, has been done on Spenser's philosophy, but it is all still in the controversial stage, and to attempt to relate one's own thesis to it is like trying to fix one's boundaries in relation to a swiftly moving train. I have, of course, always had at hand the invaluable *Reference Catalogue* of the late Dr. Ives Carpenter, and I have also in the later stages used the Handbook of Mr. H. S. V. Jones.

The volume of English criticism is incomparably less. In Professor Renwick's delightful book I have found much stimulus, but its direct bearing is less on *The Faerie Queene* than on the Minor poems, and my book was too far advanced to be much affected by the *Edmund Spenser* of Mr. B. E. C. Davis. I am deeply indebted to Dean Inge for permission to quote his *Philosophy of Plotinus* in the chapter on Spenser's philosophy. To Miss Ethel Seaton, Fellow

5

and Tutor of St. Hugh's College, Oxford, I owe some suggestions about the arrangement of the book, and much help with the appendix on Lodowick Bryskett. For the information on the differences between Giraldi and his translator I rely on her full and scholarly notes, but she is not responsible for my deductions from these notes.

JANET SPENS.

OXFORD,
August, 1934.

Contents

7

SPENSER'S FAERIE QUEENE

CHAPTER I

The Structure

Spenser's position in the poetic Pantheon is secure, but he is a god worshipped rather with the lips than with the heart. Until the last few years English critics while beginning always with formal homage, by acknowledging his place with Shakespeare and Milton at the head of our literature, have generally gone on to admit explicitly or implicitly that he wearied them. They believe that he is great, but they do not really feel it. The criticism is apt to degenerate into the citation of a few well-known passages, or into an exposition of the superficial allegory. Church's *Life of Spenser* in the '*Men of Letters Series*'— still a standard authority—devotes pages to what he regards as blemishes. Of *The Faerie Queene* he writes: 'Its place in literature is established beyond controversy, yet its first aspect inspires respect, perhaps interest, rather than attracts and satisfies . . . at first acquaintance *The Faerie Queene* to many of us has been disappointing. It has seemed . . . artificial . . . fantastic . . . tiresome.' He objects that there is much padding in the later books, and instances the marriage of the Thames and the Medway. He thinks that Spenser had exhausted or tired of his proper allegory, and so 'his poem became an elastic framework into which he could fit whatever interested him and tempted him to composition,' and preparing to praise he allows his instinctive attitude to show itself in a long list of what he regards

9

as its faults—'faults of design, and faults of execution . . .
a general want of reality, substance, distinctness and strength
in the personages of the poem . . .   Compared with contemporary drama, Spenser's knights and ladies and villains
are thin and ghost-like.'   He admits that 'our greatest poets
since his day have loved him and delighted in him' and
goes on to say that the spell lies 'in the quaint stateliness
of Spenser's imaginary world and its representatives'; in
the beauty and harmony of the style, and 'in the intrinsic
nobleness of his general aim, his conception of human life.'
But again he considers that Spenser's poetry has neither the
simplicity and directness of the Greeks, nor the finish and
felicity of the Latins, nor the massive grandeur, the depth,
the freedom, the complexity of the English drama.   He
finds his expression too abundant and complains of 'the
long spaces which the poet takes up to produce his effect.'
Even the nobility of his moral ideal has in Church's view
one serious fault—the importance given to love.

The aim I have set before me in this book is to give
back to English readers the understanding of and delight
in this great poet which thrilled his contemporaries and
early successors.   I shall not spend time on passages
which seem to me unquestionable failures (though possibly
further study might change this view), or of which the
value seems to be peculiar to Spenser's time.   But there
remains, when these deductions have been made, a whole
province of poetic experience—as it were, a lost Atlantis
drowned beneath the o'erwhelming years.   Most of *The
Faerie Queene* lies within this province, the *Amoretti*, *Epithalamion*, *Muiopotmos*, the *Hymns*, the *Prothalamion* and some
of the *Shepheards Calendar* with *Colin Clout* and *Mother
Hubberds Tale* interesting mainly for the light they throw
on Spenser the man.   Spenser's poems like Milton's are
all parts of a whole; he appears to have intended to incorporate in or to relate to *The Faerie Queene* all that he valued

in his other work.   For example, he included the substance
of the early *Epithalamion Thamesis* in the fourth book of
The Faerie Queene, not because he needed padding, as
Church thinks, but because the idea of the poem was
intimately related to the subject of that book.   Again, he
breaks off *The Faerie Queene* with an apology to Queen
Elizabeth to write his own *Epithalamion*; but I hope to show
that the shorter poem is really part of the story of Amoret,
though Spenser had not yet forged its links to the Epic
plot.   For this reason if we can interpret the mind of the
poet in *The Faerie Queene* we shall have found the secret
of Spenser's work; and this book will, therefore, be mainly
a study of *The Faerie Queene.*

The *Faerie Queene* was intended by its author to be a
philosophical poem and was so regarded by his contemporaries and immediate successors, whose appreciation of
it was so great.   According to the poet's statement in the
Prefatory Letter to the first three books, we possess very
little more than half of the whole, and none of that final
book in which the 'beginning' of the whole matter was to
be revealed.   The disadvantage of this for a philosophical
poem is obvious, but has been too much discounted; for
it is not merely the framework of the story which is lacking,
but the goal of Prince Arthur's quest, which, since the poet
'had taken in hand' to discourse at large on 'the Ethick
part of Morall Philosophie' must be equivalent to his
conception of the Good.

But I believe, further, that the whole plan of the poem,
and in part the philosophical basis, was altered, after nearly
half of what we now possess was already written, and
altered for more or less external reasons to a scheme alien
to the poet's thought and genius.   I hope to prove this
change of plan, and to indicate the lines of the original
structure.   The laying bare of this earlier ground-plan
permits us to trace a more consistent philosophic and

ethical scheme, and this new perspective in turn enables us to deal more successfully with other difficulties in the appreciation of the poet.

The history of the poem, as given to us in the Harvey-Spenser correspondence, in *Colin Clouts Come Home Again* and in the *Prefatory Letter* contains curious discrepancies within itself and with certain historical facts. As it stands it claims to be a philosophical poem based on Aristotle's Ethics, and at the same time a magnificent compliment to Queen Elizabeth. Harvey addresses his commendatory verses 'To the learned Shepheard' and Raleigh claims that Petrarch's Laura is forgotten in the blaze of glory that surrounds Spenser's Faerie Queene Elizabeth. But in the Correspondence Harvey is clearly contemptuous of the poem. 'In good faith I had once again nigh forgotten your Faerie Queene,' he writes, apparently in response to the last of very many requests for the return of the poem, and in the end cannot trust himself to speak of it. 'If so be the Faerye Queene be fairer in your eie than the nine Muses (Spenser's lost 'Comedies') and Hobgoblin runne away with the garland from Apollo: marke what I saye, and yet I will not say that I thought, but there an End for this once, and fare you well, till God or some good Aungell putte you in a better minde.'[1] The drift of his comment here suggests a poem without any classical colouring, while the commendatory verses stress the Heroic and Learned quality. He has not merely changed his mind as to the value of the poem, but appears to regard it as different in kind.

Raleigh's position as patron of the poem also suggests a change in its character between 1580, when Harvey had had it for some time, and the publication in 1590. Raleigh was in disgrace with Elizabeth when he visited Spenser, and it is clear from *Colin Clouts Come Home Again* that he

[1] *True Proper and Wittie Familiar Letters*, Oxford Spenser, 628.

hoped by bringing *The Faerie Queene* to her notice to win back her favour. But Spenser in 1579 appears to have belonged to the Leicester-Essex party and even to have been in Leicester's service, and Leicester was in trouble with the Queen apparently partly in consequence of Spenser's writings, so that it is supposed he was in effect banished to Ireland to make Leicester's peace. If, then, *The Faerie Queene* in its first state was on the same lines as it is now and as Raleigh saw it, it might surely have been used to make Leicester's peace instead of that of his rival Raleigh.

But far more important is the internal evidence. Much work has been expended over the question of the unity of structure of the poem. The lack of unity in the neo-classical sense was, we gather from Hurd and Warton, the main point of attack in the eighteenth century. Aristotle had said that an epic poem must deal with a single action: *The Faerie Queene* as it stands clearly does not. Hurd in his *Letters on Chivalry and Romance* (1742) undertakes to defend the unity, though he is not quite satisfied. His main argument is that the poem has the unity of a Gothic not that of a classical structure. He compares it with what he calls 'the Gothic method of design in gardening.' [1] In such a design 'a wood or grove' was 'cut into many separate avenues or glades. . . . These walks were distinct from each other, had each their several destination, and terminated on their own proper objects. Yet the whole was brought together and considered under one view by the relation which these various openings had, not to each other but to their common and concurrent centre.' The 'appointment of the Fairy Queen' provides in Hurd's opinion this common centre for the adventures of the various knights, and so far he is satisfied. But he thinks that Spenser was misled by classical models into attempting

[1] Extracted in Todd's *Spenser*, Vol. ii, p. clix.

'to tie his subject still closer together by one expedient of his own, and by another taken from his classical models. His own was to interrupt the proper story of each book, by dispersing it into several actions . . . in order to give something like the appearance of one action to his twelve adventures.' The other expedient was by adopting one superior character which should be seen throughout. Hurd thinks that Prince Arthur was 'but an afterthought' 'forced' on the poet 'by the *violence* of classic prejudice.'

Church also attacks the structure of the poem, but his objection is on different grounds.[1] The *Prefatory Letter* is needed to explain the poem and this is a defect. The adventures of the twelve knights were to be left 'in the air,' till at the end of twelve long books the reader should at last be told how the whole thing originated, and what it was all about. Spenser's great predecessors had all, like the good story-tellers they were, 'made their story, as it unfolded itself, explain . . . all that needed to be known about their beginnings.' Church thinks that the defect 'only came upon Spenser when it was too late to remedy it in the construction of the poem' and when part of the poem was already in the press. Raleigh, Spenser tells us, commanded him to write the explanatory letter and Church appears to assume that Raleigh's part was to point out to the poet that his plan though clear to himself could certainly not be guessed by the uninstructed reader.

Both Hurd and Church thus appear to hold that there was either an actual change of plan or an attempt to manipulate the plan at some stage in the composition of the poem. Hurd, far the more sympathetic critic of the two, feels more definitely a lack of congruity in the poem itself. Church betrays a lack of interest in and even of knowledge

[1] *Spenser, Men of Letters Series*, Chap. V.

of the poem, because having remarked that the twelve days' feast and the connection of the Quests with it, could not be gathered from the poem, he fails to press home his argument by observing that the adventures of the second and third Books are inconsistent with it, while the fourth has simply no connection with it at all.

Let us look first at Book III. The champion of that book is Britomart and she knows nothing about the Faery Queen's feast. A half-hearted attempt is made in the *Letter* to link the final adventure—the rescue of Amoret—with the feast by means of Sir Scudamour who undertakes but fails in the Quest. The *Letter* runs: 'The third day there came in a groom who complained before the Faerie Queene, that a vile Enchaunter called Busirane had in hand a most faire lady called Amoretta, whom he kept in most grievous torment, because she would not yield him the pleasure of her body. Whereupon Sir Scudamour, the lover of that lady, presently took on him that adventure. But being unable to perform it by reason of the hard enchauntments, after long sorrow in the end met with Britomartis, who succoured him and rescued his love.' Now we are told early in the fourth Book that Amoret was carried off by Busirane during the festivities for her marriage with Scudamour (*F.Q.* IV. i. 3). Yet in the *Prefatory Letter* Scudamour is at the Faery Court without her and apparently unaware of her danger till the unnamed 'groom' enters and complains to the Faery Queen. So clumsy a connection is better proof that Gloriana's behest was not the motive force of the adventure originally than no connection at all; but an example of that is provided in Book IV, where no knight is entrusted with a Quest and where indeed there is no Quest.

Book II provides the largest number of discrepancies of every sort and the *Prefatory Letter* is again at variance with the text. In the *Letter* a Palmer carrying a Babe

with bloody hands appears at the Faery Court and Guyon
is entrusted with the task of punishing the Enchaunteresse
Acrasia who had slain the child's parents. He departs,
accompanied by the Palmer as guide. But in the poem
Guyon, already attended by the Palmer, finds the dying
Mother of the babe, sees it stain its hands in her blood
and of his own volition undertakes the task of vengeance
(*F.Q.* II. i. 35).

Book I fits fairly well with the account in the *Letter*,
and in Books V and VI there are repeated references to
the Faery Queen's commission of the respective Quests
and a general reference to the scheme of the twelve days'
Feast. But Books V and VI were written after the publication of the *Prefatory Letter*. Book IV was not published
till later, but the connection with Book III is so close that
a good deal of it must have been planned, if not written
in 1590 when the *Letter* was composed.

We have, then, three Books wholly and one partially
written before, and two after, the Preface; and only one
of the first four is consistent with it, while the two later
are entirely in agreement with it. In the first group, the
adventure which fits into the scheme in the *Letter* is the
first of all, which is a significant fact. If Spenser were
somewhat hastily reconstructing his scheme he would
naturally test its coherence with what he had already
written in the first Book and perhaps re-write certain
passages. He may have forgotten the details of Books II
and III or Raleigh's urgency may have left no time for the
adjustment of the details.

These discrepancies are all connected with the twelve
days' Feast and Gloriana's appointment of the knights,
and this part may well have been suggested by Raleigh.
He probably intended the poem not only to make Spenser's
fortune at court but also to reinstate himself in the Queen's
favour. In the circumstances he would wish to make the

reference to the Queen as clear and as flattering as possible. All these great deeds must appear due to the inspiration and direct command of Gloriana herself. It is scarcely possible that this was so in the poem ridiculed by Harvey, a great tuft-hunter, and neglected by Leicester in disgrace, like Raleigh, with his royal mistress.

But the poem is also inconsistent with itself, both in incidents and thought. These discrepant incidents occur mostly in the latter part of the second and the early part of the third Book. In the ninth canto of Book II Arthur and Guyon arrive at the Castle of Alma and find her besieged by a rabble rout. They drive off these savage and formidable foes and relieve the castle. Next day Sir Guyon proceeds alone on his adventure, but Prince Arthur remains behind and has again to issue out and this time single-handed put to flight the enemy now described as being 'a monstrous rabblement of foule misshapen wights' with the heads of animals and birds of prey. When finally victorious, he is brought into the castle and laid to rest in a sumptuous bed that his wounds may be dressed. So ends the eleventh canto, and the last in the Book deals entirely with Guyon's adventure in the destruction of the Bower of Bliss, and closes with his setting forth again, alone with the Palmer. But the third Book opens with Arthur and Guyon leaving Alma's castle together.

> 'The famous Briton Prince and Faerie Knight
> After long wayes and perilous paines endured
> Having their wearie limbs to perfect plight
> Restor'd and sory wounds right well recured
> Of the fair Alma greatly were procured
> To make there longer sojourne and abode;
> But when thereto they might not be allured
> From seeking praise and deeds of armes abrode
> They courteous conge took, and forth together yode.'
>
> (*F.Q.* III. i. 1.)

The second stanza is clearly a clumsy attempt at patching up the discrepancy.

> 'But the captiv'd Acrasia he sent
>   Because of travell long, a nigher way.
>   With a strong gard, all reskew to prevent,
>   . . .
>   But he himself betooke another way.
>   To make more triall of his hardiment,
> And seek adventures, as he with Prince Arthur went.'
>
> (*F.Q.* III. i. 2.)

Now this is not even grammatically possible,—the 'they' of the last line of stanza 1 has become 'he' in the first line of stanza 2, and the obviously patchwork quality of stanza 2 suggests a version in which the defence of Alma's castle was the crowning achievement of Book II.

There is, further, a group of discrepancies in the early cantos of the third Book. Prince Arthur and Guyon meet Britomart, who is the champion of the book and Guyon attacks Britomart and is thrown. The moral of this seems peculiar. Why should the representative of Temperance be overthrown by the representative of Chastity? The incident is made more incongruous by Guyon's attitude to his defeat. He is furiously angry, and tries to attack Britomart on foot. The Palmer interferes, explaining, apparently sincerely, that Britomart's spear has magical power.

> 'And eke the Prince like treaty handeled
>   His wrothfull will with reason to assuage,
>   And laid the blame, not to his carriage
>   But to his starting steed, that swerv'd asyde
>   And to the ill purveyance of his page,
>   That had his furniture not firmly tyde:
> So is his angry courage fairly pacifyde.'   (*F.Q.* III. i. 11.)

Pacified, one cannot help feeling, like the bad temper of a spoilt child.

Of course, if we forget that Guyon is Temperance, we may regard the passage as a little piece of comic drama. From that point of view Guyon's irritation—and the means by which he is soothed—are true to life. But morally it is illogical and incongruous, and poetically it is deplorable. Such dramatic incidents are not uncommon in *The Faerie Queene* but they are generally unfortunate, and it would be true to say of Spenser, reversing the cliché about Shakespeare, that 'the dramatist in him sometimes forgets the poet.' The incongruity here again points to hurried patchwork, and the inconsistency of the incidents which follow immediately, re-enforces the argument.

Arthur, Guyon, and Britomart, having made peace, proceed on their journey together until Florimell rushes past them on her milk-white palfrey in flight before 'a griesly Foster.' The Prince and Guyon instantly give chase to Florimell, while Arthur's squire Timias follows the really dangerous quest of the Foster. On the other hand, Britomart, 'whose constant mind would not so lightly follow beauties chase', 'did stay behind' and when she found they did not return went forward on her journey alone (*F.Q.* III. i. 19). The praise of Britomart here suggests censure of both Arthur and Guyon, and again in the case of Guyon blames him for a quality incompatible with Temperance. Britomart then reaches towards evening Castle Joyous, where she finds a single knight defending himself against the six knights of the castle. She defeats the six assailants, and is then led with the knight she has rescued into the presence of the 'Lady of Delight,' who orders them to be disarmed 'in courteous wise' (*F.Q.* III. i. 42). Thus we discover that the knight—unnamed till then—is the Red-Crosse. When, however, they leave the castle together next morning, having successfully resisted the Lady's attacks, Britomart's companion is in one place called Guyon (*F.Q.* III. ii. 4). After exchange of courtesies

they finally part, and Britomart rides on till she comes to
the Precious Strand (III. iv. 12) where she overthrows
Marinell and leaving him for dead 'stay(s) not him to
lament' (III. iv. 18). Thus she overthrows Marinell the
day after Florimell's panic-stricken flight had detached
Prince Arthur and Guyon from her side. Now in canto v,
Arthur, who has parted with Guyon, finds Florimell's page
who tells him her name and that she is in love with
Marinell:

> 'But fame now flies, that of a forreine foe
> He is yslaine, which is the ground of all our woe.

> 'Five days there be, since he (they say) was slaine
> And foure, since Florimell the court for-went.'
>
> (*F.Q.* III. v. 9, 10.)

That is, Florimell started on her journey one day after
Britomart had overthrown Marinell, but she is seen in
flight by Britomart, Arthur and Guyon the day before
Marinell's overthrow.

The most interesting inconsistency in thought is connected with the Bower of Bliss. This passage—the twelfth
canto of the second Book—is probably the best known in
the whole poem and the most frequently cited as an example
of Spenser's sensuous beauty. Professor de Selincourt
writes: 'Those who blame Spenser for lavishing the re-
sources of his art upon this canto, and filling it with magic
beauty, have never been at the heart of the experience it
shadows. It is from the ravishing loveliness of all that
surrounds and leads to the Bower of Acrasia that she herself draws her almost irresistible power. When Guyon
has bound Acrasia and destroyed the Bower of Bliss he
has achieved his last and hardest victory.'[1] But in Books
III and IV we find descriptions of the Gardens of Adonis,

---

[1] Oxford Spenser, p. xliv.

which it is almost impossible to distinguish from the Bower of Bliss, and the Gardens of Adonis are at least not evil. The virtuous Amoret is 'fostered' there and 'lessoned'

'In all the lore of love, and goodly womanhood.'

It is the dwelling-place of Psyche and of Concord

'By (whom) the heaven is in his course contained
   And all the world in state unmoved stands,
   As their Almightie maker first ordained,
   And bound them with inviolable bands;
   Else would the waters overflow the lands,
   And fire devoure the ayre, and kill them quight
   But that she holds them with her blessed hands.
   She is the nurse of pleasure and delight,
And unto Venus grace the gate doth open right.' (*F.Q.* IV. x. 35.)

The Venus of this virtuous Paradise hangs over Adonis as Acrasia over her lover in the Bower of Bliss:

'There wont faire Venus often to enjoy
   Her deare Adonis joyous company,
   And reape sweet pleasure of the wanton boy;
   There yet, some say, in secret he does ly,
   Lapped in flowres and pretious spycery,
   By her hid from the world, and from the skill
   Of Stygian Gods, which doe her love envy;
   But she herselfe, when ever that she will,
Possesseth him, and of his sweetnesse takes her fill.' (III. vi. 46.)

Just so Acrasia has brought her lover to the Bower of Bliss:

'There she had him now layd a slumbering,
   In secret shade, after long wanton joyes:
   Whilst round about them pleasantly did sing
   Many fair Ladies, and lascivious boyes

   .   .   .   .   .

And all that while, right over him she hung.' (II. xii. 72, 73.)

It may be added that a being called Genius is doorkeeper both to Acrasia and to the Garden of Adonis, an unconvincing attempt being made to distinguish between them.

Now the twelfth canto of Book II is an almost literal translation from Tasso's description in the *Jerusalem Delivered* of the island of Armida. That poem was not printed till 1582. It is likely enough that Spenser may have seen part of it in manuscript, which would account for the general resemblance of the Adonis passages, though the likeness is not close enough to make any debt certain. Mediaeval literature abounds in descriptions of an Earthly Paradise. But for the Bower of Bliss Spenser must have had the *Jerusalem Delivered* in his possession. The translation is in places even closer than Fairfax's professed version of the Jerusalem—*Godfrey of Bulloigne*. The inconsistency of the moral attitude suggests that a change was made in the ethical basis of the poem between the composition of the Venus and Adonis passages and that of the Bower of Bliss.

Even had the Bower of Bliss and the Garden of Adonis been morally consistent, they might have roused suspicion by their repetitions. As it is, there is something awkward in the two descriptions of the garden in the third and fourth Books. Repetitions are indeed fairly common throughout the poem, but have been discounted by critics who insist on Spenser's redundancy. There are the two assaults on the House of Alma, mentioned above. Such a castle, it is true, might well have to sustain much more than a two-days' siege. But it is peculiar that the assailants in the second attack change their character. The enemies repulsed by Arthur and Guyon together are clearly drawn from the Irish peasants: his description in *The Faerie Queene* corresponds very closely with that in the *View of the State of Ireland*.[1]

[1] cf. M. M. Gray, *The Influence of Spenser's Irish Experiences on the Faerie Queene*, R.E.S., VI (1913), 413 *sq.*

'Thus as he spoke, loe with outragious cry
A thousand villeins round about them swarmed
Out of the rocks and caves adjoyning nye,
Vile caytive wretches, ragged, rude, deformd,
Sterne was their looke like wild amazed steares
Staring with hollow eyes, and stiffe upstanding heares.'

(*F.Q.* II. ix. 13.)

In the *View* he speaks of the wild cries with which the Irish attacked their enemies, of their disordered advance, of their creeping 'out of every corner of the woods and glinnes,' and of their ghastly appearance.[1]

In canto xi they are at first the same:

'That wicked band of villeins fresh begon
That Castle to assail on every side.' (*F.Q.* II. xi. 5.)

but almost at once their character changes. They now have a captain who divides them into several bands and appoints their stations. Then we find that they are not in human form but like mythological monsters and that they represent the temptations which attack the several senses. The castle of the body, with its gates of the senses and the enemies that attack it, was a commonplace of mediaeval devotional literature, while the realism of the foes in the earlier canto is Elizabethan. The account in the earlier canto is probably, therefore, the addition.

Perhaps less certain but more interesting are the repetitions in Book I. Like those in Book II they come towards the end of the book. Thus Duessa at the close of canto viii is 'disaraid' of her royal robes and revealed in all her native deformity (*F.Q.* I. viii. 46). This constitutes at once a fitting punishment and makes her helpless to do future harm. But in canto xii she sends Archimago disguised as a messenger to claim in the alias of Fidessa that she is the betrothed of the Red-Crosse knight, and Una's father is at first inclined to believe the claim. The

[1] *View of the State of Ireland*, Globe Spenser, pp. 632–54.

incident does provide a link between Book I and the others, but Duessa's later appearances are quite unimportant except when in Book V she stands for Mary Queen of Scots and is condemned to death by Elizabeth in the character of Mercilla; and even there the importance is not poetical.

Duessa's punishment in the eighth canto is the sequel to the release of the Red-Crosse knight from the dungeons of Orgoglio. If Duessa's punishment was originally meant to be her final appearance, then that trial was probably intended to be the last which should beset the Red-Crosse. As the poem now stands he encounters Despair in the next canto, and, though Una's intervention saves him, he is deeply affected and must go for purgation to the House of Holiness before he can slay the dragon. Now Orgoglio must stand for Pride, but the account of the castle in which he dwells and the condition of Red-Crosse when he is at last released, appear to have no obvious relation to that sin. When Prince Arthur enters he sees at first no living creature, and

> 'No man car'd to answere to his calle
> There raign'd a solemn silence over all
> Nor voice was heard, nor wight was seene in bowre or hall.'
>
> *(F.Q.* I. vii. 29.)

The Prince searches the castle without success until at last he comes to the iron door which bars the descent to the dungeon. Through the grate in this he calls:

> 'Therewith an hollow, dreary, murmuring voyce
> These piteous plaints and dolours did resound;
> O who is that, which brings me happy choyce
> Of death, that here lye dying every stound
> Yet live perforce in balefull darknesse bound?
> For now three moons have changed thrice their hew
> And have been thrice hid underneath the ground
> Since I the heavens chearfull face did view
> O welcome thou, that doest of death bring tydings true.'
>
> *(F.Q.* I. viii. 38.)

Prince Arthur breaks open the door.

> 'Where entered in, his foot could find no flore
> But all a deep descent, as darke as Hell
> That breathed ever forth a filthie banefull smell.'   (*Ibid.* 39.)

In this foul dungeon the Red-Crosse knight has been nearly starved so that his body is consumed

> 'and all his vitall powers
> Decayed, and all his flesh shronk up like withr'd flowers.'
> (*Ibid.* 41.)

The description both of the dungeon and of the condition of the prisoner reminds one of the sufferings of Christian and Hopeful in the castle of another giant—Despair. Bunyan's giant wishes to induce his prisoners to commit suicide and that in Spenser's poem is the aim of Despair in canto ix. Orgoglio's prisoner does not actually attempt self-slaughter, but he desires death :

> 'O who is that, which brings me happy choyce
> Of death . . .
> O welcome thou that doest of death bring tydings trew.'

Moreover, Duessa the paramour and accomplice of the giant being warded off by Arthur's squire takes

> 'her golden cup
> Which still she bore replete with magicke artes
> Death and dispeyre did many thereof sup,
> And secret poyson through their inner parts,
> Th' eternal bale of heavie wounded harts;
> Which after charmes and some enchauntments said,
> She lightly sprinkled on his weaker partes:
> Therewith his sturdie corage soon was quayd,
> And all his senses were with suddein dread dismayd.'
> (*F.Q.* I. viii. 14.)

This episode, then, I suggest, looks like an earlier version of the Cave of Despair, and it seems possible that Duessa's monster is the original dragon of the final canto. Prince

Arthur has a fierce struggle with him and overcomes him by the accidental display of his 'sunshiny shield' so that he

> 'Became starke blind, and all his senses daz'd
> That down he tumbled on the durtie field,
> And seemd himselfe as conquered to yield.'   (*F.Q.* I. viii. 20.)

And then this monster simply disappears. Duessa flies on foot when Orgoglio is slain and so is easily captured, but her monster has neither been killed nor otherwise disposed of. Surely the explanation is that the victory of Red-Crosse over the other dragon has been substituted for Prince Arthur's destruction of Duessa's Beast.

If this eighth canto contained the last temptation of the Red-Crosse, the destruction of the dragon, and the elimination of Duessa's power for evil, it might well have been the final canto of the book and there is a final ring about the versicle which heads the canto:

> 'Faire Virgin to redeem her deare
> Brings Arthur to the fight:
> Who slayes the gyaunt, wounds the Beast,
> And strips Duessa quight.'

Now there is other evidence that the number of the cantos in the original version was not 12 but 8.

Most critics agree with the seventeenth-century printer who gave them to the world, that the Mutabilitie Cantos seem to be part of some following book of *The Faerie Queene*. These cantos are numbered vi, vii, and viii. We must suppose that they were so numbered in the manuscript which came into the printer's hands, for the episode being complete in itself his natural course would have been to number them i, ii, and iii; or if he thought they formed a suitable close to a book of twelve cantos, x, xi, and xii. Some critics have professed to find a special type of episode in certain books, but any such arrangement is far too shadowy to suggest to the publisher that these two cantos belonged to a particular stage of an unwritten book. Other critics have regarded the two stanzas of the third canto as an envoi to the rest, but apart from the definite statement in the text, 'The viii Canto unperfite,' there is the evidence of the likeness of the matter to opening stanzas of cantos in other books, where the poet reflects on the task he has just finished and gives his judgments on questions raised by it.

But if the numbering is impossible as the printer's own invention, it is at least surprising even for the poet, unless he intended the book to have only eight cantos, when it would be perfectly natural. The episode, although complete in itself, must be related to the rest of the Book and this could be done in one canto.

The cantos apparently were twelve because there were to be twelve books. It does not, of course, follow that because there were only in the first plan eight cantos in each book there were only eight books. But Spenser had certainly a passion for symmetry and, when we find independent evidence that the number of books was originally eight, the testimony of cantos and books is mutually supporting.

There is only one piece of direct evidence in favour of an original eight books plan, but it is very surprising. When the Red-Crosse knight is invited by Una's father to 'devize of ease and everlasting rest' (*F.Q.* I. xii. 17, 18), he replies that he has still six years in which he has vowed to serve the Faerie Queene. Now it is natural to assume that the Quest just accomplished has taken one year. That gives seven years that the Red-Crosse must serve in all. But there must be some reason for the selection of the number. One would expect each knight either to return to Fairyland after achieving his own Quest or to remain on duty until all twelve have been brought to a successful issue. Neither six nor seven years as the scheme now stands gives any sense. There would be no place in the poem to give an account of the knight's final happiness. But if there were to be eight books only, the seven years of the Red-Crosse's service would be explained. There would then be seven quests and the conclusion of the whole matter would be given in the eighth book.

Such an arrangement allows adequate space for the framework which was to hold the separate books together. The scheme of the *Prefatory Letter* does not. There Prince Arthur is to represent Magnificence 'because it is the perfection of all the rest and conteineth in it them all,' and there are to be twelve other knights representing 'xii other virtues,' each quest apparently recorded in a separate book. But in the twelfth book, which is the last, is to be recorded the beginning of the whole business and presumably the accomplishment of Prince Arthur's quest. It looks as if Spenser were at least a book short. Moreover, as has been frequently pointed out, Holiness cannot possibly be regarded as one of Aristotle's virtues. Attempts have been made by critics to equate it with one of the qualities in the *Ethics*, but Spenser himself makes no such effort. If then it was to be added, it makes fourteen virtues. In fact, however, Aristotle seems to be an afterthought. Prince Arthur is as unlike Aristotle's Highminded Man as any two heroes could well be. He is liable to be inflamed with desire, he is pitiful and affectionate, while the High-minded Man is none of these things. Moreover, when in any book Aristotle's particular doctrines are illustrated, the poetry immediately disappears, leaving us to plod along the dry highway of ethical commonplace.

Harvey's contempt for the original *Faerie Queene* suggests that its plan was popular. He blames the poet for preferring Hobgoblin to Apollo. But popular literature was impregnated with mediaeval religious symbolism. Now the House of Holiness in the first Book, the House of

Alma in the second, the majority of the evil forces against which the knights fight, and the miraculous weapons on which their victories depend are all connected with the allegorical language of the mediaeval sermon-writer.[1] That language itself seems to have been developed from Neo-Platonic mysticism allied with folk-lore and fairy-tale, and by the sixteenth century it was the material chiefly of the humbler sort of village preacher. Owst shows that Bunyan was probably greatly indebted to such sources, and links which have puzzled scholars between Spenser and Bunyan are probably really the debts of both to the preachers. Now perhaps the most frequently recurring theme of this sermon literature was naturally the war of the soul against the seven deadly sins, and if we examine the first four books of *The Faerie Queene* we shall see that far more is said of the temptations of the champions than of the virtues which these champions represent. In Book IV, for example, the Book of Friendship, there is more fighting than in any other. Even the titular heroes who embody the conception of Friendship are shown to us chiefly in a tourney to the death against each other. The real subject of the Book, in fact, appears to be Wrath. Book III becomes far more of a unity when we see it as the representation of the sin of lechery. Guyon's temptations in Book II fall into two main groups, the first group being represented chiefly in canto vii—the account of the Cave of Mammon, the Court of his daughter Ambition, and the garden of Proserpine; and the second in the Bower of Bliss. If we put aside the Bower of Bliss and all that leads up to it as an addition, we are left with Avarice as Guyon's crowning temptation.

The sin of Book I is at first sight more obscure, but it is particularly significant. We have seen that there appear

[1] cf. Owst, *Literature and Pulpit in Medieval England*, p. 79. Cambridge, 1933.

to be two very important episodes showing the Red-Crosse a prey to Despair. When we find, further, that of the three Paynim Brethren, Sansfoy, Sansloi and Sansjoy, it is the last who is the Red-Crosse's most formidable enemy, we are driven to assume that there is some special significance in this stressing of a tendency to melancholy. Such a tendency is not now regarded as a serious sin, but in mediaeval times melancholy leading to inertia and in extreme cases to suicide was under the name of *accidie* one of the recognized Deadly Sins. By Elizabeth's day the much less pregnant term Sloth had been substituted in the usual catalogue, and Spenser nowhere uses the word *accidie*. But the late sixteenth and early seventeenth centuries were much preoccupied with the subject. They regarded the sufferers from it as at once in a highly dangerous spiritual state and as intensely interesting. It was the favourite pose of fashionable young men. Hamlet is the supreme treatment of it in literature, but most of the dramatists of the day are interested in it. I suggest that the first Book of the original *Faerie Queene* treated of the sin of *accidie*.

We have then, in the first part of *The Faerie Queene*, four of the seven deadly sins depicted in the more important passages of the four several books; those sins being much more elaborately and powerfully represented than the virtues, which are opposed to them, and which are personified in the titular heroes of the respective books. The alteration which made these personified virtues the centre each of a book was probably part of the reconstruction on the basis of Aristotle's *Ethics*.

The nature of the debt to Aristotle suggests that Spenser did not borrow directly from the Greek, but by way of modern translations. J. C. Bryce, in a letter to the *Times Literary Supplement* of August 10, 1933, shows grounds for holding that the *De Regimine Principum* of Aegidius Columna Romanus is probably the ultimate source of the

Aristotelian doctrines in *The Faerie Queene*, but that the direct debt may well be to the Spanish adaptation of the *De Regimine* by Juan Garcia de Castrogeriz. Again, the form of the reference in the *Prefatory Letter* to the Cyropaidia suggests some connection, otherwise extremely probable, with Giraldi's *Three Discourses of Civill Life* which has a long account of the training of Cyrus. The English version of these *Discourses* was, of course, given to the world by Spenser's friend, Lodowick Bryskett. Such books, at least, fit more easily into the Aristotelian references in *The Faerie Queene* than Aristotle's own work. Now Spenser could read Greek: he almost certainly learned to read it at the Merchant Taylors School, and it is incredible that anyone with such a gift for language as he, coming up to the University with some knowledge of it, should have failed in seven years' residence to develop that knowledge. Moreover, Bryskett in his introduction to the *Discourses* says explicitly that Spenser was 'perfect in the Greek tongue,' and had offered Bryskett to help him in acquiring it. The use, then, of a modern translation points to the insertion of the Aristotelian colouring when Greek books were not at hand, and not to a time when the poet, lately come from the University, was moving in bookish circles in England. He would be able to borrow such books from Bryskett, who was anxious to make acquaintance with Greek philosophy but did not know the language and approached it by means of such translations the paucity of which in English he deplores. His words imply that he had the Italian books in his possession: he would not be likely to possess books he could not read.

The reference then to Aristotle's *Ethics*, like Gloriana's commission of the champion knights, belongs to the reconstruction. Was Hurd right in the belief that Prince Arthur was also an afterthought? The present writer suggests that on the contrary Prince Arthur belonged to the original scheme. The poem was certainly always called *The Faerie Queene*, and if the Feast at which the Quests were appointed is a late insertion we are left without any connection between Gloriana and the substance of the poem unless she is the goal of Prince Arthur's Quest. He is much more important in the first two than in the later books, releasing Red-Crosse from Orgoglio's castle, killing the giant and subduing the Beast in Book I, canto viii; and coming to the rescue of Guyon when he is 'laid in swoon' after his sojourn in the cave of Mammon, and repelling the enemies of Alma in Book II, canto viii. He drops out of the last three cantos of these Books.

The difficulty about Prince Arthur is simply that he does not fit into the Aristotelian scheme. He is not like the 'magnificent man'; he requires a thirteenth book and his relation to the Faerie Queene becomes superfluous when the champions of the first three books all achieve their crowning adventures without his help. On the other hand, the adventures of the eighth and ninth cantos of the first two books are turned from defeat into victory by his aid. This suggests that Prince Arthur belonged to the original shorter poem and was the centre round which it was built. The poem was to consist of eight books of eight cantos each and Prince Arthur's quest of the Faerie Queene was its main theme. As the poem was a moral allegory the Faerie Queene must have been equivalent to the Good or the Heavenly Beauty, and Prince Arthur must be the soul. Seven of the books were to be devoted to the conquest of the seven Deadly Sins by the hero and the last was to describe Prince Arthur's realization of his vision. To this original plan belongs the greater part of the first three books; much of the fourth, small fragments of the fifth, much of the sixth, and the whole of the Mutabilitie Cantos. This with the additions to Books I and II covers all the best poetry in the work, and the fact that it does so, and that it all fits into what has been suggested as the original plan, strengthens the argument for that plan.

The increase in the number was probably partly effected, as in the case of *Paradise Lost*, by division of the existing cantos, but more was certainly done by padding. The last four cantos of the first Book were simply added. They include the second Despair episode, the visit to the House of Holiness, the fight of Red-Crosse with the dragon and his marriage to Una. As suggested above the first and the third of these are elaborations of earlier treatments of the same incidents, while the second and the last may be modifications of matter intended for the final Book. The marriage of Red-Crosse after his refusal to abide in Una's land confuses the moral allegory. So does the helplessness of Una's parents against the dragon. Truth must be the child of God himself, but Una's father cowers in his castle till relieved by the victory of the Red-Crosse and is uncertain what to believe about Duessa's accusations against the champion. I suggest that the marriage so beautifully sung was originally that of Arthur to the Faerie Queene and that she is the Heavenly Beauty of the *Hymns*. The original dragon was the Beast of canto viii and had nothing to do with Una's parents.

The case of the second Book is simple so far as three cantos are concerned. The last was added from Tasso. The defence of the House of Alma was duplicated, and a chronicle of the Kings of Briton and the Elfin Emperors, wearisome to the modern reader, at once provided another canto and afforded an opportunity for some rather confusing genealogies apparently meant to placate Elizabeth. But according to my theory, Spenser still lacked a canto. I suggest that canto v was added. It is suspiciously short —thirty-eight stanzas instead of the usual forty-five or fifty—and it falls into two halves neither of which appears

to be quite in the right place.   The second part describing
Cymochles in the Bower of Bliss is taken from the *Jerusalem
Delivered*; partly from the tenth Book where Armida's
island is first introduced, and partly from the passage
used for the final canto.   It was probably added at the
same time.   The first twenty-four stanzas belong to the
tale of Pyrochles and Furor, which was begun in canto iii.
This may be an instance of division, but if in the original
scheme Wrath was treated in Book IV, then all the part
of Pyrochles and Furor would belong to that book.

Book III appears to have been too much altered to per-
mit of tracing the original scheme,[1] but Book IV, although,
as Mr. Notcutt argues,[2] a sort of architectural unity has
been imposed on it, retains traces of the ruined building
from which its materials have been drawn.   Prince Arthur
controls events in cantos viii and ix and then disappears.
Canto x is a complete monologue in which Sir Scudamour
tells the tale of his winning of Amoret, a tale which clearly
ought to come in Book III.   Canto xii is a fairly clear
case of division.   It has only thirty-five stanzas, less than

[1] I believe that the Third Book was to deal originally with the stories
of the twin-sisters Belphoebe and Amoret, and that Britomart is an afterthought and has usurped much of Belphoebe's adventures—notably the
rescue of Amoret.   It is artistically wasteful to make no use of the twin-
sisters' ignorance of each other's existence; and the ethical significance would
be much clearer if Amoret were saved from the evil pangs of passion by
her other self, her twin-sister Virgin Chastity.   Even as the poem stands
it will be found that the plot gains in coherence if Amoret, not Britomart,
is made the central figure.   To make the story complete the tenth canto
of Book IV—the winning of Amoret—should be inserted where it naturally
belongs, after the description of her fostering in the Garden of Adonis.
The first half of canto i (the indecorous quarrel of Guyon with the knight
of Chastity) and all of cantos ii and iii (the story of Britomart's love for
Artegal) would then go out.   But more room is required, and I believe,
for this and other reasons, that the tale of Florimell and Marinell belongs
to the final Book.

[2] *The Faerie Queene and its critics.*   Essays and Studies of the English
Association, Vol. 12.

any other in the whole poem, and it is simply the ending of the single story of the loves of Marinell and Florimell. It may not belong to Book IV originally—it probably does not—and it is certainly too slight to stand by itself.

An even more obvious case of transfer from another book is canto xi—the marriage of the Thames and the Medway. It must be a re-writing of the early *Epithalamion Thamesis*, and is one of the most beautiful and characteristic passages in the whole poem. But it is out of place here. The figures in it are neither human beings nor moral abstractions, but personifications of natural forces and features; and the poet at one point stresses the fact. Now the personages of the Mutabilitie Cantos are, although grander and more universal, of something the same order of being. Canto xi of Book IV, I suggest, was intended for the earlier part of the same book as the Mutabilitie Cantos. And that book must have been the last. The Mutabilitie Cantos deal not with problems of individual ethics, but with the laws of the universe out of which ethical laws arise. The crowning book of any philosophical poem must give such an ontology and relate to it the ethical theory. But the Mutabilitie Cantos belong to the older, the eight Book scheme, and they are easily to be interpreted and only to be interpreted by the light of Neo-Platonic doctrines. We may, therefore, draw the conclusion that the older poem, the poem as it was born of the poet's own development was Neo-Platonic in tendency. The treatment of Aristotle's doctrines is superficial because it was alien to the poet's genius and hastily adopted for some external reasons.

The question arises of the date at which the changes in Spenser's plan could have been made. The twelve days' feast and the inception of the quests at it might have been, and probably was, suggested to the poet not long before the writing of the *Prefatory Letter*. The inconsistencies between the poem and the *Prefatory Letter* can only be so explained. It is noticeable that the Red-Crosse knight, in the stanza (I. xii. 18) in which he speaks of the six years' service still due from him to Gloriana, explains that the service is to be

'Gainst that proud Paynim King, that makes her teene'

a line which suggests a mistress hard pressed by enemies rather than one holding high festival. Moreover, in Book II, canto ii, Guyon explains that his adventure was initiated, not at a twelve days' feast, but at one on

'The day that first doth lead the yeare around'

and his account here corresponds with what happens in the poem, though not with the Preface. It may be noticed that Guyon is the only one of the patron knights who belongs to the order of Maydenhead, and as such bears the image of Gloriana on his shield, and that in the fourth Book Sir Satyrane is the chief champion of the order. Thus a special reason is offered for Guyon's commission by the Faerie Queene, which does not apply to the others.

But if the twelve days' Feast as the 'beginning' of the history might scarcely have been thought of before the necessity for the Preface was urged, the rearrangement of the adventures round knights each of whom represents a virtue, and the raising of the number of the cantos to twelve, must obviously have taken several years, particularly when the poet was a busy civil servant living in a disturbed country. Spenser might have started the reconstruction shortly after Gabriel Harvey's contemptuous return of the manuscript early in 1580, but by the end of that year he was acting as Lord Grey's secretary in Ireland, and from that time till a few weeks before his death his professional duties kept him there, except for a few short visits to London.

The most probable date for the beginning of serious

work is 1582. In that year Lord Grey was recalled and henceforth the poet's offices seem to have been of a more independent nature. From that time too began his association with Lodowick Bryskett, with whom he seems to have discussed his work and who was in a position to lend him Italian books, both philosophical and poetic. Most important of all, in that year was published the *Jerusalem Delivered* from which the Bower of Bliss was translated. On the other hand, it is likely that the first three books were nearly in their present shape by 1588, when Abraham Fraunce quotes stanza 35 of Book II, canto iv, as coming from that place.

CHAPTER II

The Philosophic Basis

The evidence suggests that the Mutabilitie Cantos were intended for the three last of the final Book. We should expect, therefore, to find in them some indication of the poet's basic conception, and if the poem is philosophical as it claims to be, and as the poet's contemporaries clearly believed it was, something of an ontology. It is significant that critics who deal with Spenser's thought always seem to find their path leading them to these cantos. The statement of the poet's position is necessarily incomplete, since of the last canto we have only a fragment, but the general direction of the lines of his thought is sufficiently clear. Their fundamental importance has been obscured because they are Neo-Platonic in tendency, and the references to Aristotle in the *Prefatory Letter* have misled students.

It is very possible that the poet never read any complete work of Plotinus, the great Neo-Platonist with whom he has affinity; although as he read not only Greek and Latin but Italian, the first modern language into which the Greek philosophers were translated, he may have done so. But a knowledge of Neo-Platonic doctrines was in the air. Already when Spenser was a Cambridge undergraduate a party to which Gabriel Harvey belonged had repudiated Aristotle's logic, and in 1549 a statute enjoined a lecturer to substitute readings in Pliny or Plato for those in Aristotle. The great age of Cambridge Platonism comes after Spenser's death, but the inspiration of a new intel-

lectual hero was upon Cambridge already when Spenser
went up in 1569. Moreover, Platonism and Puritanism
appear to have been associated, while the followers of
Aristotle belonged rather to the older Church. It was
almost inevitable that Spenser should have begun life as
a Platonist. On the other hand Leicester, whom Spenser
served at a later date, was Chancellor of Oxford and in
Oxford the doctrines of Aristotle had maintained a much
stronger hold. Spenser may well have heard in the circle
round Leicester and Sidney discussion in which the claims
of Aristotle were forcibly set forth. If we may trust
Bryskett's account in the introduction to his translation
of Giraldi's *Discourses*, the effect was to leave an impression
that neither philosopher was entirely satisfactory. Bryskett
takes his knowledge from Spenser himself, and he holds
that the great need of English thought is a synopsis of
Ethical philosophy such as it is the 'great happiness of
the Italians' to possess 'who have in their mother-tongue
late writers that have, with a singular easie method, taught all
that which Plato or Aristotle have confusedly or obscurely
left written.'

It was to Neo-Platonism that the Italian writers turned
to reconcile Greek philosophy with Christian doctrine and
it would have been natural for Spenser to follow in their
footsteps even if he had not had a natural affinity with
Neo-Platonist doctrine. Spenser's age was eclectic, and
poets in all ages take from the thought of the time what
is akin to their own inner world. For the consistency
of a poetic philosophy is not the logical consistency
of the professional philosopher. It is a harmony of
emotional experience, not a train of syllogistic reasoning.
Now Spenser discovers with the great Neo-Platonist Plotinus
a natural affinity. That philosophy came home to him
for two reasons: on the one hand, Plotinus differed from
Aristotle's main conception by the stress he laid on the

upward striving of the soul; on the other, he accepted the world of sense as good, while the logical issue of Platonism is to reject it. Plotinus's combination of the two doctrines is apt to seem inconsistent to the predominantly rational man, but it is a commonplace of experience to the poet, and his ontology must somehow justify the data supplied by his own fullest being. The Mutabilitie Cantos deal with this antinomy and suggest a resolution due ultimately at least to Plotinus.

The main matter of the cantos—there is a digression which supports my interpretation and to which reference will be made later—is the attempt of the Titanesse, Mutability or Change, to dispossess the Olympian gods and make herself supreme ruler of Earth and Heaven. She claims, indeed, that her apotheosis would be a mere recognition of the facts. Now according to Dean Inge this question was the form which the ultimate problem of philosophy took for the earliest Greeks.[1] 'The relations,' he writes, 'of the eternal and the temporal, of reality and appearance, of spirit and matter, or to use the favourite antithesis of Plotinus of Yonder (ἐκεῖ) and Here (ἐνταῦθα) constitute the first and last problem of philosophy. To the earliest Greek thinkers the greatest crux was the reconciliation of *change* and *permanence*.' He appears to mean that these four antinomies are but different expressions of the same problem. Spenser adopted the earliest form, but the other antitheses are at different times present in his thought. Mutability identifies (stanza 47) her power with that of Time and in answer to the claim of Jove that the gods 'from their heavenly cell' 'pour that virtue' 'that moves' all things, replies with contemptuous refusal to believe in the 'Yonder' at all.

[1] Dean Inge, *The Philosophy of Plotinus*, Vol. I, p. 124. London, 1929 (3rd edition).

'The things
Which we see not how they are mov'd and sway'd
Ye may attribute to yourselves as Kings,
And say they by your secret powre are made:
But what we see not, who shall us persuade?'
(*F.Q.* VII. vii. 49.)

Thus the Temporal, Mutability or Change meant to him the infinite variety of the physical universe of matter, 'appearance,' the miraculous world of what Wordsworth calls 'outward circumstance' blasphemed by the prosaic as evil delusion.

Spenser's adoption of Mutability as the personification of the physical universe was influenced mainly no doubt by aesthetic reasons. Like Shelley he is intensely attracted by things in motion, by the fugitive, by moving water, flickering shadows, by human figures dancing or in flight. It is characteristic of him that his successful large pictures are of processions, pageants which defile before the poet's eyes, not great assemblies into which he enters. They have unity, but it is a unity of rhythm and movement, not of co-existence in space. But the aesthetic preference is reinforced by his philosophy. Like Plotinus he saw succession in time as of the essence of the physical universe. The physical universe is a copy of the Eternal world, but with a difference. 'Every distinct idea Yonder (that is, in the Eternal world) becomes a finite purpose (or process) Here' [1](that is, in the world of sense). Every attribute of God when transformed to the temporal world 'becomes an activity of his existence.' Again, 'Because this act of creation is willed, and willed as a process, there must be an interval between the inception and conclusion of the process. This interval is Time.' [2]

This conception of time explains the myth of the Virgin Hours who guard the gate through which the Olympian

[1] Inge, *The Philosophy of Plotinus*, I, p. 182.   [2] *Ibid.*, p. 184.

gods issue into the lower world. There is a certain vagueness and confusion in Spenser's presentation of the gods, and at the trial their claims are feebly stated. There can be no doubt, however, that they are 'the ideas of the Yonder,' 'the attributes of God.' Now in Hesiod the Virgin Hours, who open the gate of this lower world are the daughters of Jupiter and Themis. Spenser makes them the daughters of Jupiter and Night. Todd in his great edition of Spenser notes the alteration, which must have a meaning.[1] Hesiod's myth makes the Hours the offspring of Divine law and primitive human custom. Todd appears to think that Spenser means they are the children of day and night. This is probably one aspect of the truth, but Spenser had the mediaeval conception of truth as being like a vein of precious metal running steadily through every stratum of existence. Elsewhere in *The Faerie Queene*, Night stands for primeval chaos or matter; Duessa, for example, addresses her as

'most auncient grandmother of all,
More old then Jove, . . .
Which wast begot in Daemogorgons hall,
And sawst the secrets of the world unmade.' (*F.Q.* I. v. 22.)

The Hours, then, are the children of the union of the Divine Principle with Matter, because they are created by the Divine Principle when about to realize Itself in process in this lower world, that is, in matter: and the Olympian gods are the attributes of the Divine Principle issuing into this secular world. That is the meaning of Nature's final judgment:

'I well consider all that ye have sayd
And find that all things stedfastnes doe hate
And changed be: yet being rightly wayd
They are not changed from their first estate;

---

[1] Todd, Vol. VII, pp. 237–8.

But by their change their being do dilate,
And turning to themselves at length againe,
Doe worke their own perfection so by fate:
Then over them Change doth not rule and raigne;
But they raigne over Change, and doe their states maintaine.'

(*F.Q.* VII. vii. 58.)

The choice of the name 'Nature' for the judge of the question is a little confusing to the modern mind, as is also the form of a legal trial. For the verdict is not a statement of equity but of fact, and Nature is a personification of the laws of existence. Spenser holds that the fundamental characteristic of this temporal existence is change. But change is not evil. Throughout the myth the beauty of the Titanesse is insisted on. When she makes her claim before Jove in his Heaven, the gods are astounded at her loveliness:

'Whilst she thus spake, the gods that gave good ear
To her bold words, and marked well her grace,
Being of stature tall as any there
Of all the gods, and beautiful of face
As any of the goddesses in place,
Stood all astonied; . . .   (*F.Q.* VII. vi. 28.)

Again Jove takes in hand his lightning that he may 'thunder-drive the Titanesse to Hell.'

'But, when he looked on her lovely face,
In which, faire beames of beauty did appeare,
That could the greatest wrath soone turne to grace,
(Such sway doth beauty even in Heaven beare)
He staide his hand.'   (*Ibid.,* 31.)

The beauty clearly implies that Mutability is good and it is interesting to note how near she comes to success. Not only does Nature appear to hesitate before giving her sentence, but in the first stanza of the fragmentary eighth canto, the poet himself echoes her doubt:

'When I bethinke me on that speech whyleare
    Of Mutabilitie, and well it way!
    Me seemes, that though she all unworthy were
    Of the Heav'ns Rule; yet very sooth to say,
    In all things else she beares the greatest sway.'   (VII. viii. 1.)

In *Muiopotmos* there is a direct statement of the delightful-
ness of change.   He says of his hero the Butterfly Prince
in his happy morning:

    'And evermore with most varietie
    And change of sweetmess (for all change is sweete)
    He casts his glutton sense to satisfie.'   (*Muiopotmos*, 177–9.)

Succession in time is a condition of variety and in so far
good, but the inalienable defect of the secular process is,
that the beautiful moments may not co-exist, so that the
poet is made to

            'loathe this state of life so tickle
    And love of things so vaine to cast away;
    Whose flowring pride, so fading and so fickle,
    Short Time shall soon cut down with his consuming sickle.'
                            (*F.Q.* VII. viii. 1.)

It is, then, perfectly consistent that he should turn with
longing to that Eternity

            'when no more Change shall be
        But stedfast rest of all things, firmely stay'd
        Upon the pillours of Eternitie.'   (*Ibid.*, 2.)

The two stanzas were to be an introduction, it can hardly
be doubted, to a final canto in which the Eternal Loveliness
was to be revealed: the Mutabilitie Cantos are the poet's
interpretation and vindication of the world of sense.

    Some critics find Spenser too sensuous, even fleshly,
but the charge—for it amounts to a charge—is generally
supported by reference direct or indirect to the Rubens-
like description of the Bower of Bliss, and that description
is not truly characteristic of Spenser.   This pageant of

the temporal world cited by Mutability is less dependent
on its source and *is* characteristic and profoundly different
from Tasso's work.   Tasso appears to think the senses
evil and the poet in him seizes the opportunity of a pro-
fessedly wicked scene to revel in fleshly loveliness.   Spenser,
on the other hand, is like Rupert Brooke, 'the great Lover,'
so that anything intensely itself has an irresistible attraction
for him.   Wordsworth, as Professor de Selincourt has
pointed out, manifests in the earlier form of *The Prelude*
a mystic feeling for the verb 'to be'; this feeling is what
he later calls 'the sentiment of being'—a passionate excitement in face of anything which, however momentarily,
utterly and exclusively *is* itself.   It is this passion that
accounts for what has repelled some readers in Spenser—
his full descriptions in many places of the purely ugly.
As he watches the pageant which unrolls itself before him
all human preference for what is apparently lovely is
burned out of him by the disinterested passion for all that
exists.   Take the description of the seasons who lead
Mutability's Masque:

'So forth issued the seasons of the yeare;
　　First, lusty spring, all dight in leaves of flowres
　　That freshly budded and new bloomes did beare
　　(In which a thousand birds had built their bowres
　　 That sweetly sung to call forth Paramours)
　　And in his hand a javelin he did beare,
　　And on his head as fit for warlike stowres
　　A guilt engraven morion he did weare
That as some did him love, so others did him feare.'
(F.Q. VII. vii. 28.)

· · · · ·

'Lastly came Winter cloathed all in frieze,
　　Chattering his teeth for cold that did him chill;
　　Whilst in his hoary beard his breath did freeze,
　　And the chill drops that from his purpled bill
　　As from a limbeck did adown distill.

In his right hand a tipped staffe he held,
With which his feeble steps he stayed still;
For he was faint with cold, and weake with eld,
That scarse his loosed limbes he hable was to weld.'   (*Ibid.*, 31.)

To the poet, spring with its blossoming bird-bowers is no more worthy of note than old winter with his purple nose from which water drops.   This impartiality and yet ardour of observation exorcises the evil element of sensuality.

But there is another characteristic of Mutability's pageant which marks the affinity of Spenser's thought to that of Plotinus, and one more fundamental.   All the figures in the masque—the Seasons, Months, Hours, Night and Day and Life—are, like Death itself, mere creations of our minds.   The details of the pictures—winter's breath frozen on his beard, October 'tottie of the must' are concretely vivid, but the seasons and the months themselves are abstractions—ideas or names round which our constructive thought groups these pungent but fleeting impressions and by this grouping gives them 'a local habitation and a name.'   As we listen to the lines:

'Yet is he nought save parting of the breath;
Ne ought to see, but like a shade to weene,
Unbodied, unsoul'd, unheard, unseene:'   (*F.Q.* VII. vii. 46.)

the phantoms dissolve before us with a sigh into thin air. With them truly *esse est percipi.*

Spenser has a natural predilection for objects held in solution as it were by an idea, and his favourite pictures are made of lights and shadows that arrange themselves momentarily into significant images, but the doctrine of Plotinus appears to have provided here as elsewhere the basis of Spenser's thought.   Plotinus realized that 'The Naturalist is not, as he supposes, describing what he sees, he is interpreting it.   He is translating sensuous impressions into the language of human thought.   Without

this labour of the human mind, there would no doubt be
something left, but it would not be a world.' [1]

Corroboration of Spenser's conscious acceptance of the
doctrine of Plotinus is afforded by the way in which it
links the digression in the Mutabilitie Cantos with the rest
of the matter. In this digression Spenser accounts for
certain changes in the country round Kilcolman by a
frankly playful myth telling of the wrath of Diana with
her nymph the river Molanna. The nymph having be-
trayed Diana is 'whelmed with stones' and this accounts
for the condition of the river-bed. The constructive fancy
is seen at work. A passage in Browning's *Paracelsus*
throws light on the connection of the digression with the
main subject of the Mutabilitie Cantos. Browning has
described the evolutionary process up to man, and goes on:

'man once descried, imprints for ever
His presence on all lifeless things; the winds
Are henceforth voices, wailing or a shout
A querulous mutter or a quick gay laugh,
Never a senseless gust now man is born.
The herded pines commune and have deep thoughts

. . . . .

the peerless cup afloat
Of the lake-lily is an urn, some nymph
Swims bearing high above her head: no bird
Whistles unseen, but through the gaps above
That let light in upon the gloomy woods
A shape peeps from the breezy forest top
Arch, with small puckered mouth and mocking eye.'

(*Paracelsus*, V.)

Browning's 'shape with small puckered mouth and mocking
eye' is surely parallel to Spenser's Faunus 'breaking forth
in laughter' at the joyful sight of Diana's unclothed loveliness. Both poets draw from the doctrine that man's
consciousness is a necessary element in the full being of

[1] Inge, *Plotinus*, Vol. 1, p. 148.

the universe around him, a half-playful argument for the reality of mythical beings who incarnate his subtler reactions to Nature.

Thus while the Mutabilitie Cantos are the poet's defence of the world of sense, they are at the same time an attack on materialism. His whole point of view assumes a body of doctrine like that of Plotinus as a background. 'In the Enneads,' writes Dean Inge, 'the sensible world is the creation of the universal Soul, through the medium of Nature which is its moving power . . . all (Nature's) activity comes from Soul.' [1] And again, 'the natural world, which we see with our eyes, is spiritual throughout and instinct with life . . . though its spiritual characters are faint and hard to trace. In looking for them, we make as well as find them.' [2] And the world of sense is both created by soul and held in being by its desire towards it. Dean Inge quotes from the eighth Book of the third Ennead a passage in which at first playfully it is asserted that the whole temporal universe, 'all living beings not only rational but irrational, and all vegetables and the earth which produces them, aspire to contemplation and look to this end, and attain to it as far as in them lies.' [3] 'All life,' quotes Dean Inge, 'is a kind of spiritual vision,' and goes on, 'every natural thing, he holds, in its own way longs for the Divine and desires to share in the divine life as far as it can.' 'The Good moves the whole world because it is loved.' [4] Thus it will be seen the whole basis of Plotinus's philosophy both ethical and natural is this aspiration of the universe towards the vision of perfection. For 'the Soul (here the individual self-conscious self) is in truth a stranger among the things of sense.' Its characteristic is the presence in it 'of unfulfilled desire.' 'It realizes itself by turning towards its principle . . . and the more

[1] Inge, *Plotinus*, Vol. I, p. 155.   [2] *Ibid.*, p. 161.
[3] *Ibid.*, p. 156 *sq.*   [4] *Ibid.*, p. 161.

(it) lives in the light of Spirit turned towards that which is above itself, the more creative it becomes.' [1]

Now this description of Soul corresponds closely with what Spenser tells us of Prince Arthur in the poem. Passages of the *Prefatory Letter* agree, but again the references to Aristotle are a little confusing. In both preface and poem, however, Prince Arthur from the moment of his vision of the Faerie Queene is possessed by an inextinguishable desire for her. 'In that Faerie Queene,' writes Spenser, 'I mean glory in my general intention,' and it cannot be doubted that she stands for the supreme loveliness—the Sapience of the *Hymn* of Heavenly Beauty, the 'Principle' of Soul. All the feats which Prince Arthur performs—and originally it is clear he was to achieve, or at least to assist in the most arduous adventure of each book—he performs by virtue of his quest of Gloriana, as the Soul becomes 'more creative' the more it is 'turned towards' that which is above itself. But this Arthur who strives towards the mark of the prize of his high calling is inconsistent with the Prince who is explicitly identified in the Preface with Magnificence, 'for that (according to Aristotle and the rest) it is the perfection of all the rest, and conteineth in it them all.' For Magnificence has no need to strive and the element of desire is alien to Aristotle's High-minded Man.

The philosophy of Plotinus with its tripartite division both of man and the universe at large into body, soul and spirit affords a key to much that has been held inconsistent, or at least disconnected, in Spenser's poetry. The praise of Venus in the Garden of Adonis and the attitude there to the physical passion of the lovers has been felt to be discontinuous with the poet's attitude, not merely in the *Hymns* to Heavenly Love and Beauty, but also in the earlier *Hymns*, where the poet himself thought his emotion

[1] Inge, *Plotinus*, Vol. I, p. 204.

on a lower plane. But the love of these three passages
is that which is respectively appropriate to body, soul and
spirit. Each is good in its degree, or perhaps in regard
to the two lower, one should say—capable of goodness.
Hence the sympathetic treatment of Venus and of the
Garden of Adonis. Venus is clearly justified in her claim
to Diana:

'We both are bound to follow heavens behests
And tend our charges with obeisance meeke.' (*F.Q.* III. vi. 22.)

And the beneficence of her influence is indicated in her
final conciliation of the too-fierce Phoebe:

'So her she soone appeased
With sugred words and gentle blandishment,
Which as a fountaine from her sweet lips went
And welled goodly forth, that in short space
She was well pleasd' (*Ibid.*, 25.)

and with her damsels joined in the search for the lost
Cupid. Here again Acrasia and the Bower of Bliss, which
we are apt to take as a representation of Venus herself
and her dwelling-place, has obscured Spenser's direct statement that the simple physical attraction is good in its kind.

The love of the two first *Hymns* is the love appropriate
to the soul of Plotinus's Trinity, that of the third to the
spirit. It may be noted that the love of this third *Hymn*
is the Agape of Professor Nygren's analysis in 'Eros and
Agape,' while that of the two first is Eros. Agape is the
love of the higher for the lower, beneficent, gracious:
Eros is the love of the lower for the higher. The Heavenly
Beauty of the last *Hymn* represents that to which the upward striving soul only half-consciously seeks to unite
itself and which is the full and effortless possession of spirit.
Aesthetically the interest of the four *Hymns* is the great
range and variety of emotion within the apparently narrow
frame.

CHAPTER III

Symbolism

'The generall end of the (Faerie Queene) is to fashion a gentleman or noble person in vertuous and gentle discipline,' writes Spenser in his *Prefatory Letter*; and in the Prologue to Book VI he tells us 'Vertues seat is deep within the mind' and calls on the Muse of Poetry to reveal to him 'the sacred noursery of vertue' 'Where it in silver bowre does hidden ly' and to guide him 'In these strange waies,' the waies of 'this delightfull land of Faery.' Faery Land then is the mind, the inner experience of each of us, and the subject of *The Faerie Queene* was the same as that of Wordsworth's projected *magnum opus* more than two centuries later—the apprehension, description and organization of the inner world.

It may, however, be objected that in the Prologue to Book II the poet had explicitly identified Faery Land with England.

'And thou, O fairest Princesse under sky,
In this faire mirrhour maist behold thy face,
And thine owne realmes in lond of Faery,
And in this antique Image thy great auncestry.'

But this objection has little force. The passage appears to be part of the hasty revision to make the poem redound to the glory of Elizabeth and appears to be incoherent with the preceding stanzas. However that may be, it is like all the political allegory frankly superficial—an occasional ornament, a fanciful flourish. Spenser's mind ran

in places on mediaeval lines, and the fourfold interpretation of the Scriptures to which he was accustomed in the
mediaeval devotional literature with which he was obviously
familiar, made it seem natural to him that his poem, if
essentially true, should also be consistent with many aspects
of experience. The historical parallels had for Spenser
the argumentative force of a fine metaphor, and as with
such metaphors, the parallel is only intended for that
particular context. A proof of this is, that a character in
the poem may at different places represent different historical
persons, or an historical person and an abstract entity; while
on the other hand one historical person may be 'shadowed'
in different characters in the poem. Spenser himself points
out that Elizabeth is 'shadowed' both in Gloriana and in
Belphoebe, while Gloriana stands not only for Elizabeth,
but for 'Glory in the general intention.' Similarly, Faery
Land stands both for England and for the inner world of
mind, and poetically 'the general intention' is always far
the most important. The superficiality here of the particular identification of Faery Land with England is
proved by the drift of the preceding stanzas. In those
the poet is occupied with the question of the truth of
that world.

> 'Right well I wote most mightie Soveraine
> That all this famous antique history.
> Of some th'abundance of an idle braine,
> Will judged be, and painted forgery.
>
> .   .   .   .   .
>
> Sith none that breatheth living aire does know,
> Where is that happy land of Faerie
> Which I so much do vaunt, yet no where show,
> But vouch antiquities, which no body can know.'

And the poet bases his argument for the existence of
'that happy land,' on the thought of how little we really
know of the universe:

'dayly
Many great Regions are discovered
Which to late age were never mentioned.
Who ever heard of th' Indian Peru?
Or who in venturous vessell measured
The Amazons huge river now found trew?
Or fruitfullest Virginia who did ever vew?'

Now since

'All these were, when no man did them knowe
Why then should witlesse man so much misdeeme
That nothing is, but that which he hath seene?
What if within the moones faire shining spheare?
What if in every other starre unseene
Of other worldes he happily should heare
He wonder would much more; yet such to some appeare.'

(*F.Q.* II, proem.)

All this fine poetic enchanting to bring about 'the sus-
pension of disbelief' in the unseen is irrelevant if Faery
Land and all it contains is merely a sort of anagram for
the England of Spenser's day.

Spenser's subject was, then, the same as Wordsworth's
in *The Recluse*. The famous passage in the Preface to
The Excursion shows that Wordsworth was comparing
himself with both his two great predecessors. He quotes
from Milton and goes on:

'Urania I shall need
Thy guidance, or a greater Muse, if such
Descend to earth or dwell in highest heaven!
For I must tread on shadowy ground, must sink
Deep and aloft ascending, breathe in worlds
To which the heaven of heavens is but a veil.
All strength—all terror, single or in bands,
That ever was put forth in personal form—
Jehovah—with his thunder, and the choir
Of shouting angels, and the empyreal thrones—
I pass them unalarmed. Not Chaos, not

The darkest pit of lowest Erebus,
Nor aught of blinder vacancy, scooped out
By help of dreams can breed such fear and awe
As fall upon us often when we look
Into our Minds, into the Mind of Man—
My haunt, and the main region of my song.
Beauty—a living Presence of the earth,
Surpassing the most fair ideal Forms
Which craft of delicate spirits hath composed
From Earth's materials—waits upon my steps;'

Spenser is almost certainly here chief of the 'delicate spirits,' as Milton is indicated by the quotation, the reference to his Muse and the splendid allusion to the substance of *Paradise Lost*. Wordsworth feels an essential likeness between the subject of his projected poem and those of his great predecessors, but he feels his matter to be greater, because theirs was expressed 'in personal form,' in 'fair ideal Forms,' and he implies that with such embodiment falsehood entered.

In this Wordsworth is typical of his age, and of the whole nineteenth century, and it is this difficulty about the expression which explains the lack of sincere appreciation of Spenser throughout the nineteenth century and up to our own day. Spenser is essentially an Elizabethan, and the Elizabethans tended to utter their more intense emotions through the imagery of human figures: the men of the nineteenth century had been trained to accept the expression of theirs through the imagery of inanimate nature. 'Strong imagination,' says Theseus, 'if it would but apprehend some joy . . . comprehends a bringer of that joy.' A vivid mental experience seemed to the Elizabethans like another personality affecting them from without. Personification was not a fully conscious mental activity, but an involuntary result of the combination of intense emotion with an inherited habit of mind. Ruskin remarks that in the Middle Ages 'the virtues came at last to be con-

fused with the saints; and we find in the later litanies
St. Faith, St. Hope, St. Charity and St. Chastity invoked
immediately after St. Clara and St. Bridget.' Abstractions
were warm with personality in those times, but Ruskin
is speaking for his own generation and the two centuries
which preceded him when he remarks that 'Personification
is apt to disturb the belief in the reality of the thing
personified.'

To the nineteenth century reality was material, unconscious and impersonal: the visible tangible physical world
was the only certain existence. The imagery and form
of expression in poetry necessarily followed this belief.
Not that the poets in the depths of their poetic consciousness could so deny the spiritual, but their function, and
particularly the function of a poet like Wordsworth, is to
mediate between the general mental world of their day and
the 'Eternal Verities.' Inevitably and without deliberate
intention their imagery adapted itself to the sincere convictions of those they addressed, convictions which they
to some extent shared. Coleridge, gazing on Mont Blanc,
feels his 'Soul as in her *natural* form rise vast to Heaven.'
'Huge and mighty forms that do not live like living men' are
the incarnation of Wordsworth's most intimate experiences.

To the Elizabethans, on the other hand, reality was a
personal God fully reflected in miniature in man and
faintly and partially in the different elements of the physical
universe. As representative of the personal God, man
was at once the explanation and the *raison d'être* of the
physical universe. He was at the fixed centre of that
universe and the magnificent pageantry of planets and
stars moved round him and for him. The revolution in
scientific thought at the beginning of the seventeenth
century which reduced the earth to the position of an
insignificant planet among many others revolving round
the sun, also dethroned earth's chief creature, man. For

centuries the physical universe had been explained in terms
of man; for three centuries science and philosophy were
to attempt to explain man in terms of the physical universe.
A passage from Wordsworth's *Prelude* (xii. 231), the detail
of which suggests that the Romantic poet's recollection
was stimulated by a passage in *The Faerie Queene*, will
illustrate the difference in method that resulted from a
difference in habit of thought. The passage describes an
experience of his early childhood. (The 1805–6 version
of the poem says 'he was not six years old.') He had gone
riding among the hills accompanied by an old servant,
from whom by some accident he was temporarily separated.
He lost his way and became frightened. Then he passed
the spot where a gibbet had once stood and where in the
turf someone had cut the name of a murderer who had
once hung there:

'The monumental letters were inscribed
In times long past; but still from year to year,
By superstition of the neighbourhood,
The grass is cleared away, and to this hour
The characters are fresh and visible.
A casual glance had shown them and I fled,
Faltering and faint, and ignorant of the road:
Then, reascending the bare common, saw
A naked pool that lay beneath the hills,
The beacon on the summit, and more near,
A girl who bore a pitcher on her head,
And seemed with difficult steps to force her way
Against the blowing wind. It was, in truth,
An ordinary sight; but I should need
Colours and words that are unknown to man
To paint the visionary dreariness
Which, while I looked all round for my lost guide
Invested moorland waste, and naked pool
The beacon crowning the lone eminence,
The female and her garments vexed and tossed
By the strong wind.'

Here the gibbet and the fact that he had lost sight of his companion had no doubt aroused the melancholy mood, but the mood itself finds perfect expression in the 'visionary dreariness' of the moorland waste, 'the naked pool' and 'the beacon crowning the lone eminence.' Even the figure of the girl is curiously dehumanized by the epithet 'female.' (It has been altered from 'the woman' of the 1805–6 version.) Wordsworth's emotion is embodied in the landscape.

In the first Book of *The Faerie Queene* the Red-Crosse knight deceived by Archimago has left Una, who

> 'Forsaken, wofull, . . . as in exile
> In wildernesse and wastfull deserts strayd'   (I. iii. 3.)

to seek him.

> 'Till that at length she found the troden gras
> In which the tract of peoples footing was
> Under the stepe foot of a mountain hore;
> The same she follows, till at last she has
> A damsel spyde slow footing her before
> That on her shoulders sad a pot of water bore.'   (*Ibid.*, 10.)

The girl flies from Una and her attendant lion

> 'And home she came whereas her mother blynd
> Sate in eternall night: nought could she say
> But sudden catching hold, did her dismay
> With quaking hands, and other signes of fear.'   (*Ibid.*, 12.)

There is, of course, a somewhat bald and obvious allegory here, of superstition put to flight by Truth, but its poetic value lies chiefly in its suggestion of the mental experience of one gone astray in the twilight of superstitious instinct and wandering among the grey chill shadows that cling to the by-ways of the mind. The emotion is the same as that of the Wordsworth passage. Una's poetic superiority to the other companions of the champions—Guyon's Palmer, Artegall's Iron man—is that, besides representing religious truth both as a dynamic force in the historical world of events and as a quality in the character of the Red-Crosse knight, she is also sometimes herself a heroine and so simply a conscious being catching, co-ordinating and reflecting the various elements surrounding her. Here she corresponds to the child poet and both represent the soul passing through this terror-thrilled region of super-stition, aware of, but uncontaminated by it. The dreary little vignette of the girl on the 'troden path' with the indication of hopeless resignation in her attitude, the following dumb terror and her flight to her blind mother in the dark cottage is a picture also of the kind of conditions—abject poverty, dreariness and ignorance—in which superstition moves in the external world. But that is only one facet of the episode and not the most important poetically, for here as throughout *The Faerie Queene* the 'general intention' is the poet's main concern and that here is the utterance, evocation and synthesis of the various filaments of emotion which go to make up this City of Dreadful Night.

This was Wordsworth's purpose also. In his work, narrative and description exist simply as formulae of incantation by which magnificent emotional presences may be evoked. The curious un-English detail of the girl carrying the pitcher of water on her head suggests that the actual biographical incident has been coloured by the Spenser passage in the *hinterland* of Wordsworth's memory. In any case the poets are depicting the same mental ex-perience—a gloomy twilight of the mind in which primitive forms move uneasily: but Wordsworth expresses this sense of desolation in terms of the landscape with the human figure as a mere element in it; Spenser while touching in the 'hore mountain' and 'the troden path' finds utterance mainly in the attitudes and actions of the imbecile girl and her blind mother, who literally embody his emotion.

The change of attitude, to which I have referred, came

about the end of the first third of the seventeenth century
when the discoveries of the astronomers began to reach
the minds of the ordinary man of intelligence.   Carew,
writing (about 1640) elegiac verses on John Donne, speaks
with contempt of the introduction of mythological beings
into poetry.   William Browne, Drayton and the Milton
of Horton days can still create bodies for emotional per-
ceptions, which, while clearly visible to the mind's eye,
are yet radiantly metaphysical.   On the other hand, the
curious lapses of imagination in Milton's treatment of his
spiritual Beings in *Paradise Lost* is perhaps a symptom
of the growing materialism.   In his drafts of *Paradise
Lost* as a drama the evils which afflict Adam after his fall,
and Faith, Hope and Charity which comfort him, are
personified.   It was perhaps one of the chief advantages
of the epic form that save for Sin and Death these figures
disappeared, while it is significant of the eighteenth-century
attitude to the subject that Johnson apparently failed
entirely to appreciate that magnificent episode.   He points
out the incongruities in it similar to those in the treatment of the angels, and then goes on: 'This unskilful
allegory appears to me one of the greatest faults of the
poem; and to this there was no temptation, but the author's
opinion of its beauty.'   It is clear that Johnson did not
feel the temptation.   All through the eighteenth century
personification is dead-alive, a convention of literature
which, with rare exceptions, freezes what it touches.
Blake and Shelley, both out of sympathy with their times,
have regained the power.   Shelley is, indeed, of all later
poets most like to Spenser—the *Adonais*, the *Witch of
Atlas*, the *Cloud*, the *Skylark* are the work of a nineteenth-
century Spenser.   The last act of the *Prometheus Unbound*
gives a picture of a reign of peace and bliss in a form
that would fit perfectly into the Mutabilitie Cantos.

But Shelley had no successor till the end of the century

when Rossetti, with the great poet's instinctive anticipation
of the movement of explicit thought in science, turned
towards individual emotion as the one important element
in existence and in doing so created a new world of personifications.   Rossetti left no single great poem because
to him reality consists of an infinite number of emotional
moments jostling each other in a universe that is 'without
form and void,' but these emotional moments have all 'the
human form divine.'

And the scientists of our own generation are leading us
back to the human consciousness as the only reality of
which we can have other than symbolic knowledge; back
to personality as the dynamic force.   'It is,' writes Professor Eddington, 'of the very essence of the unseen world
that the conception of personality should dominate it. . . .
We have to build the world out of symbols taken from our
own personality. . . .   After exhausting physical methods
we returned to the inmost recesses of consciousness, to the
voice that proclaims our personality.'   This is characteristic of the trend of scientific thought, and the attitude of
the moral philosophers is similar; the finest ethical doctrine
of the age depends on the conviction of the supreme value
of individual consciousness.   The revival of the study of
Spenser contemporaneously with this change in the ontology
of scientists and philosophers is not an accident.

But there was a curious paradox in the nineteenth-
century attitude.   In spite of men's dislike and distrust
of personifications, their whole structure of thought was
based—and ours still is—on abstract 'fictions' like the
figures in Euclid's demonstrations.   We use such Platonic
ideas as beauty, ugliness, truth, force, space, though we
struggle to empty them of the substantiality which the
instincts of our primitive minds attach to them.   We
have recently become aware of it.   'Our thinking,' says one
writer, 'would be fluid, if it were not that by fictions we

obtain imaginary standpoints and boundaries by which to gain control of the flow of reality.' We have evolved a mythology of our own, which is so interwoven with our methods of thought that we are unaware of it. We think that we are dealing with scientific fact when we talk of mind, matter, silence, vacuum—but in truth we are creating entities, which are quite as much personifications as any of the figures in eighteenth-century poetry. 'The most sober investigator in science,' writes Vaihinger, 'cannot dispense with fictions; he must at least use categories.' A reviewer in the *Times Literary Supplement* compared the relation between thought-symbols and meanings to the story of 'a great malignant spirit' which could only become active by 'snatching up some cloth or sheet and literally embodying itself in it.'

But for the nineteenth century these fictions must remain ghosts—colourless, indefinite, abstract, while the men of the Renaissance and the true Elizabethan required concrete images. Just as we find it almost impossible to deal freely with the conceptions of time and space, as we cannot disentangle them from our three-dimensional life, though our children may find the idea of space-time obvious; so the Elizabethans saw moral qualities and mental experiences steeped in colour and confined by form. They thought and felt in pageants, but in our days 'the visions have grown pale in human sensibility.' This entanglement of the Elizabethan mind in sensuous detail explains why so much of the impression of Spenser's finest figures —the emotional quality—is given through a description of their raiment. Take our first introduction to Una:

> 'A lovely lady rode him fair beside
>   Upon a lowly asse more white than snow
>   Yet she much whiter, but the same did hide
>   Under a robe that wimpled was full low
>   And over all a black stole she did throw.'   (I. i. 4.)

Compare this with the description of Belphoebe's dress which fills several stanzas and is more effective to suggest her charm than the generalized hyperbole on her face:

> 'She was yclad, for heat of scorching aire
> All in a silken camus lyly whight
> Purfled upon with many a folded plight,
> Which all above besprinkled was throughout
> With golden aygulets, that glistened bright,
> Like twinckling starres, and all the skirt about
> Was hemd with golden fringe.'   (II. iii. 26.)

Una's is a holy loveliness, an angelic moonlike radiance; Belphoebe is more royal, and though 'clad in the beauty of a thousand starres' she suggests rather the effluence of sunbeams.

Most significant of all, the impression of Prince Arthur's personality at his first appearance is conveyed through a long description of his armour. Part of the description was borrowed by Marlowe to decorate his ideal Tamburlaine, and the changes he makes and the difference in the personality suggested by these changes illustrate the effectiveness of the method. This is Prince Arthur:

> 'At last she chaunced by good hap to meet
> A goodly knight fair marching by the way
> Together with his squire, arrayed meet;
> His glitterand armour shined far away,
> Like glauncing light of Phoebus brightest ray;
> From top to toe no place appeared bare,
> That deadly dint of steele endanger may;
> Athwart his brest a bauldrick brave he ware
> That shynd, like twinkling stars, with stones most pretious rare.
>
> His haughtie helmet horrid all with gold
> Both glorious brightnesse, and great terror bred;
> For all the crest a Dragon did enfold
> With greedie pawes, and over all did spred

His golden wings; his dreadful hideous head
Close couched on the bever, seemed to throw
From flaming mouth bright sparkles fiery red
That sudden horror to faint harts did show
And scaly tayle was stretcht adowne his backe full low.

Upon the top of all his loftie crest,
   A bunch of haires discolourd diversly,
   With sprincled pearle, and gold full richly drest
   Did shake, and seem'd to daunce for jollity,
   Like to an almond tree ymounted hye
   On top of greene Selinis all alone,
   With blossomes brave bedecked daintily;
   Whose tender locks do tremble every one
At every little breath, that under heaven is blowne.'

                   (*F.Q.* I. vii. 29, 31, 32.)

Compare this with the passage in Marlowe where the
same simile is used, with a difference, of the plumes dancing on the helmet:

   'Thorow the streets with troops of conquered kings
   I'll ride in golden armour like the sun,
   And in my helme a triple plume shal spring
   Spangled with diamonds dancing in the aire,
   To note me Emperor of the three fold world.
   Like to an almond tree ymounted high
   Upon the lofty and celestial mount
   Of ever greene Selinus quaintly dect
   With blosmes more white than Herycina's browes,
   Whose tender blossoms tremble every one
   At every little breath that thorow heaven is blowne.'

        (*Tamburlaine,* Part II, Act iv, sc. ii, 11, 114.)

If we set the two descriptions side by side like this, we
seem to find something material, almost vulgar in Marlowe's gold and diamonds and 'troops of conquered kings.'
Tamburlaine's boast 'thorow the streets . . . I'll ride in
golden armour like the sun' fails to catch the note of
spiritual excitement that we hear thrill in Spenser's line

'His glitterand armour shined far away,' a line which
may have suggested Milton's 'farre off his coming shone.'
Tamburlaine's 'conquered kings' introduce the note of
human strife and fury and the hero is himself involved in
these passions; while the dragon on Arthur's helmet inspires horror in the beholder, but the Prince is enfolded
in a majestic calm. Again, Marlowe's modifications of the
almond-tree simile, slight as they are, make a significant
difference in the impression of his hero. He had given
him a triple plume for the single plume of Prince Arthur,
as a symbol that he was Emperor of 'the threefold world,'
and therefore the almond tree could not be 'all alone.'
So Spenser's lovely line 'On top of greene Selinis all alone'
becomes 'Upon the lofty and celestial mount Of ever
greene Selinus quaintly dect,' and the whole spiritual value
of the simile is lost. For we associate Arthur himself
with the lovely solitary tree in the holy calm of its green
hill and a sense of purity and ardour in high adventure
mingles with our thought of him.[1]

The Elizabethan predilection for the expression in human
form of its experience culminated naturally in drama.
But drama, although the chief, was not the only literary
species developed from this seed, and Spenser at least has
suffered from the subconscious expectation of dramatic
interest. Fundamentally such interest is alien to his art,

---

[1] The commentators are a little puzzled by 'greene Selinis' but assume
it should be Selin*us* and that the poets have in mind the reference in Virgil
(*Aen.* III, 705) to the city 'palm-girt Selinus.' But both in Spenser and
in Marlowe a hill and not a town is indicated, and the almond tree would
not be alone if it were in a grove of palms. The name Selinus is said to
come from the parsley which grew profusely near the site—parsley which
was used for the crowns of the victors in the sacred games. Prince Arthur
is, of course, the Christian soldier who has put on the whole armour of
God, and he is also the destined victor in 'the race that is set before us'
who will receive a heavenly crown. It is, then, of the parsley and not of
Virgil that Spenser is thinking, and I suspect some kind of association with
the hills of the Holy Land.

though we do find imbedded in *The Faerie Queene* incidents which not only might play their part in drama, but which actually suggest parallels in Shakespeare's plays, and may possibly have come from Spenser's lost nine comedies. Passages, for example, in the adventures of Braggadocchio bear some likeness to those of Falstaff. The immediate surrender of Sir John Colevile of the Dale to the fat knight as soon as he hears his name reminds one of Trompart's submission to Braggadocchio. Falstaff (*Henry IV*, Pt. II. IV. iii.) describes the incident to Prince John, 'I, travel-tainted as I am, have, in my pure and immaculate valour, taken Sir John Colevile of the Dale, a most furious knight and valorous enemy. But what of that? he saw me and yielded,' which is no more than the truth. Falstaff goes on to threaten that if his services are not acknowledged he will have a ballad written with his picture 'on the top on't, Colevile kissing my foot.' In *The Faerie Queene* Trompart, seeing Braggadocchio armed and riding on Guyon's horse, 'fell flat to grounde, for feare.' 'And crying Mercy lowd, his piteous hands gan reare.' Braggadocchio much pleased 'with big thundering voyce revyld him lowd,' but on the further entreaties of Trompart grants his life and commands him:

> 'Therefore prostrated fall
> And kisse my stirrup.'

Again Braggadocchio's excuse for his cowardly retreat before Belphoebe, that he knew instinctively she was a goddess, is the same as Falstaff's for not attacking Prince Hal disguised as a Highwayman, that his lion's instinct forbade him to touch the true Prince.

The flight of the adulterous Hellenore with Paridell (*F.Q.* III. x.) and the agony of her miserly and jealous husband Malbecco reminds us inevitably of Jessica's flight from Shylock carrying much of his wealth with her, and of Shylock's outcry about his ducats and his daughter. Earlier the picture of Hellenore sitting rapt, listening to Paridell's story of his adventures, recalls Othello's description of his wooing of Desdemona. Spenser makes an episode (*F.Q.* II. iv. 24–28) of the same intrigue as Shakespeare uses in the serious plot of *Much Ado*, and Shakespeare may have taken it from him rather than from the Italian. Todd points out the very curious parallel between the image used by Spenser to tell of Paridell's casting off of Hellenore and Othello's threat that he will do the same to Desdemona 'if he do prove her haggard.'

Apart from parallels of this sort we have occasionally human touches, which suggest dramatic capacity. Such is the delightful picture of Britomart's old nurse putting the love-sick girl to bed:

> 'And the old woman carefully displayd
> The clothes about her round with busie ayd;
> So that at last a little creeping sleepe
> Surprisd her sense: she therewith well apayd,
> The drunken lampe downe in his oyle did steepe,
> And set her by to watch, and set her by to weep.'   (III. ii. 47.)

There are other incidents of this sort, but not very many, and where, as here, they are felicitous, they are used, not dramatically to illustrate the peculiar characters of Glauce or of Britomart, but to indicate an element in the universal emotional experience. Spenser's subject here is the birth of love. He wishes to depict a love, ardent, gallant, romantic, ideal, and yet very definitely of the flesh, not the love of a particular woman whose character gives to her experience these qualities. Such an episode as this plays the part in Spenser's technique of the kind of simile, which T. S. Eliot points out Dante used—a vivid little picture to get the note clear. Spenser has need of the note of tenderness, and of the sense of primitive human instincts, and the physical bond between Glauce and her nursling, and the old woman's tears—an expression of half-conscious emotion—gives exactly the quality he needs.

We have another little dramatic episode in canto xii. of Book I in the comic description of the behaviour of the crowd after the slaying of the dragon:

> 'Some feard, and fled; some feard and well it faynd;
>   One that would wiser seeme, then all the rest,
>   Warnd him not touch, for yet perhaps remaynd
>   Some lingring life within his hollow brest,
>   Or in his wombe might lurke some hidden nest
>   Of many Dragonets, his fruitfull seed;
>   Another said, that in his eyes did rest
>   Yet sparckling fire, and bad thereof take heed;
> Another said, he saw him move his eyes indeed.
>
> One mother, when as her foolehardie chyld
>   Did come too neare, and with his talants play,
>   Halfe dead through feare, her litle babe revyld,
>   And to her gossips gan in counsell say;
>   How can I tell, but that his talants may
>   Yet scratch my sonne, or rend his tender hand?
>   So diversly themselves in vaine they fray;
>   Whiles some more bold, to measure him nigh stand,
> To prove how many acres he did spread of land.'
>
> (I. xii. 10, 11.)

The description here is almost Addisonian in its delineation of the mixture of superficiality and pose with naïve self-revelation and vacant wonder characteristic of an English crowd. It gives the dragon concrete reality as nothing else could do.

It may be questioned, however, whether the passage is not poetically a mistake, and, as a rule, incidents simply dramatic occur in *The Faerie Queene* only when the poet's inspiration is running low. The attempt to interpret his figures as ordinary persons in a drama is irrelevant and disastrous. There is, it is true, some likeness between Spenser's women and those of Shakespeare's last plays. Una, Florimell and Pastorella are sisters of Imogen, Miranda, and Perdita, but both chronology and the evidence of the logical development of his thought show that it was Shakespeare's art which underwent a sea-change and approximated to that of his contemporary. In his last plays, life seems more fluid, more ethereal, less dominated by man's conscious will and purpose, and yet woven into a coherent pattern by some creative Force of which man's poetic imagination is the earthly shadow. The young Shakespeare had been intensely excited by sensuous experiences, and his *Venus and Adonis* is an expression of the awakening artist's excitement in presence of the physical world. But as Chapman knew, 'The sense is given us to excite the mind,' and his line justifies and explains the whole group of mythological and narrative poems of which *Venus and Adonis* is the best known. In Shakespeare's case at least, such work is only a preparation for his true task, the painter's charging of his palette. The next stage was the human and dramatic world of Julius Caesar, of Hamlet, of Othello, of Macbeth. These great figures are intensely alive and responsible for what befalls them, though behind and beneath them we are aware that 'there are more things in Heaven and earth than are dreamt of in your philosophy.' But in the last plays men are little-doing, much-suffering—'such stuff as dreams are made on'— driven on by the winds of Time, through a universe that is no longer solid and fixed, but of the airy substance of a fantastic tale.

Spenser, on the other hand, may have begun with frankly dramatic work. It is possible that the links with Shakespeare's plays, to which reference has been made, are material worked over from the lost *Comedies*. So far as we know he never passed through the merely sensuous stage, or if he did his exercises in it have not come down to us.   In the work we have he never deals so much with the sensuous fact as with the mental translation of the fact—with the use which the soul's faculty makes of the impact and stir of the physical sensation; and he is more excited by the infinitely various web which man has woven to adorn and clothe the physical universe than by the simple physical facts themselves.   He cared more for the artificial than for nature, because in the artifact the sensuous element is more visibly held in solution by the concept. And he was haunted by a bewildering complexity of emotion, and needed an elaborate instrument to utter its music.   He could not use primary colours, but must deal with dyes brought from strange vats and fabrics made ethereal and translucent to thought by the fading of their tints under the suns of forgotten centuries, stained with blood and tears, so that by magical accident they fall into the pattern of his dream.   When, for example, Glauce tries by charms to save her nursling from the pangs of hopeless love, her incantations are reminiscent of the girl whom Theocritus saw in a Sicilian garden under the moonlight trying to ease her intolerable yearning, and the incantations themselves stir the primeval memories which linger near the springs of passion.

Thus, on the one hand, Spenser's thought is steeped in sensuous detail, so that for him there is no really abstract thinking; men, he thinks, 'should be satisfied with the use of these days, seeing all things accounted by their showes, and nothing esteemed of, that is not delightfull and pleasing to commune sense' (*Prefatory Letter*).   But on the other hand the details of the physical universe become translucent from the pulsing light of varied human experience which is seen behind it.   His 'haunt and the main region of (his) song' is the inner life of man and it is described in the symbolism of human figures clothed in raiment iridescent with innumerable associations. His art is a development of the mediaeval.

To his own generation Spenser was 'the new poet'; to their successors he is 'the poets' poet,' and it has not always been realized that the two titles mean much the same. The Elizabethans merely meant that the mantle of poetry had fallen on a new prophet, and one who had inherited to the full all the gifts of his predecessors. Neither Spenser nor his contemporaries thought of his work as new in the sense that Wordsworth and Coleridge thought of theirs, when they brought out the *Lyrical Ballads*. Wordsworth's art, indeed, is naïve; it is to Spenser's as the earliest form of picture-writing is to the latest development of hieroglyphic. The representative images linger like a haunting fragrance round the symbols the Elizabethan uses: if we mistakenly try to translate them back into the full primitive form the result is a distasteful incongruity, which amounts at times to incoherence. This is, for example, the explanation of the swan-brides of the *Prothalamion*. The silver purity of the swan symbols enables the poet to give directly—in concrete image—his sublimated conception of the girl-brides. Later, when their bridegrooms come down to the water's edge to receive them, we are intended to see only maidens round whom hovers the radiance of a lovely mystic and withdrawn existence.

The dangers of the method are seen fully in the work of Spenser's spiritual sons, Giles and Phineas Fletcher. Not once but many times in the course of a poem they forget the physical symbol from which they started in pursuit of the idea for which that symbol stood, so that when they again return to earth they find themselves in an entirely different region, and the reader is completely bewildered. An obvious example of this occurs in the description of Sin the Portress of Hell's gate in *The Apollyonists* of Phineas.

She is first described as 'a shapeless shape . . . nor nothing, nor a substance' and the poet fills the stanza with this sublime conception of sin as non-being. But then he returns to his story and Sin becomes a woman described in some detail as beautiful in front, though hideous behind. Milton was clearly inspired by the passage, but here as elsewhere he brings order out of the chaotic suggestiveness of the Fletchers' conceptions. He retained the second part for his picture of Sin, but made the first the basis of his image of Death:

> 'The other shape—
> If shape it might be called that shape had none
> Or substance might be called that shadow seemed
> For each seemed either.'

Such confusion as Fletcher's, however, occurs nowhere in Spenser, and the slight grotesqueness of the swan-brides is probably intentional. For Spenser is a fully conscious artist inheriting, but using with complete freedom and originality, a highly developed medium.

CHAPTER IV

'From breath of outward circumstance'

In Wordsworth's statement of his subject in the passage from *The Recluse*, he explains that the inner experiences which form his majestic subject come either 'from breath of outward circumstance or from the soul an impulse to herself.' 'Outward circumstance' means for Wordsworth mainly physical and inanimate nature—what Shelley in his *Mont Blanc* calls 'the external universe of things'—but also external events. Spenser appears to have made the same distinction, and confusion has been caused by the failure to recognize it. Except in one or two cases when the reference to the physical world was unmistakable, all the figures and episodes in the poem have been supposed to have ethical significance. The quality of the poetry has been lost on both sides. Figures which represent the natural world are curiously degraded by the forced application to them of inappropriate human standards; while the few obvious examples of nature allegory not only appear like excrescences upon the poem, but lose their more delicate and imaginative associations.

The clearest example of nature poetry is the description of the marriage of the Thames and the Medway in the fourth Book. It must be an adaptation of the lost early poem *Epithalamion Thamesis* and was perhaps written in some form before even *The Shepheards Calender*. It is natural then that it should belong to Spenser's poetry of the world of sense. Its technique is most easily understood when studied in connection with that of the April

Eclogue of *The Shepheardelends Car*, by common agreement the crown of that work. That is a conventional
design, a piece of highly sophisticated art, which yet
manages to retain a dewy quality. The gloss of E.K. is
certainly inspired if not written by Spenser himself, and
by it the poet offers not so much an interpretation of the
words and allusions as of the poetic method. Without
the gloss, for example,

> 'The redde rose medled with the white yfere
> In either cheeke depeincten lively chere:'

might easily be passed over for a trite description of Elisa's
complexion, but the gloss stresses the reference to the roses
of York and Lancaster and so gives us the clue to the
interpenetration of symbolism and natural representation,
corresponding to some extent to a modern artist's interpretation of a physical object by geometrical and rhythmical
lines. Linked with this is the deliberate grouping together
of flowers that do not all bloom at one season—roses with
daffodils, primroses, and violets—in the Queen's coronet.
They are brought together out of time and space to produce an effect that would elude more direct expression.
The names of the flowers are a sort of charm by which
particular complex groups of memories may be evoked:

> 'Bring hether the Pincke and purple Cullambine,
>   With Gelliflowres;
> Bring Coronations and Sops in wine,
>   Worne of Paramoures:
> Strowe me the ground with Daffadowndillies,
> And Cowslips, and Kingcups, and loved Lillies:
>   The pretie Pawnce,
>   And the Chevisaunce,
> Shall match with the fayre flowre Delice.'   (*S.C.*, April Eclogue.)

Most of the names are slightly deflected from the more
common forms, sometimes to get the particular musical
note required at the place—daffadowndilly and pawnce—

sometimes to blur the representative image, so that the real flowers, with their fragrance as of cottage gardens, stiffen miraculously into conventional entities and then blossom anew in a sort of Platonic or Virgilian Heaven where the true name of the fleur-de-lys is found to be flower of delight. Coronation is a country form of carnation, and combines with the peasant note the quality of a conventional pattern regally flourished. Chevisaunce is not a name for any known flower and it is unlikely that Spenser connected it with any, but the word, 'blind' in the gardener's sense, has a hint of heraldry and chivalry and carries on the arabesque effect of the whole stanza, thus 'match- (ing) with the fayre flowre Delice.' Spenser uses chevisaunce in *The Faerie Queene* to mean something like 'deeds of chivalry.' Its more usual contemporary meaning was quite prosaic. Compare its use in the May Eclogue (ll. 92, 93).

> 'They maken many a wrong chevisaunce
> Heaping up waves of welth and woe.'

In the marriage of the Thames and the Medway also, the poet is intoxicated with his medium—with words of beautiful sound and elusive associations as of delicate perfumes. He is playing, as Shelley is playing in *The Witch of Atlas*, with the implements of his craft—sweet sounds and visions and odours 'clipt in a net a love-sick fairy had woven from dew-beams while the moon yet slept.' In the Spenser passage there is a wealth of names and memories of rivers and mythological beings, which only now and then become clear and lovely pictures. We see Neptune and his Queen

> 'Faire Amphitrite, most divinely faire,
> Whose yvorie shoulders weren covered all,
> As with a robe, with her owne silver haire,
> And deckt with pearles which th' Indian seas for her prepaire.'
>
> (*F.Q.* IV. xi. 11.)

Before them Triton blows

> 'his trompet shrill
> For goodly triumph and great jollyment,'

while Arion crowned goes 'playing on the watery plaine'
(*F.Q.* IV, xi. 24) as herald of the Bridegroom who is

> All decked in a robe of watchet hew,
> On which the waves glittering like crystal glas,' (*F.Q.* IV. xi. 27.)

are 'cunningly enwoven.'   But most beautiful of all is the
Bride, the lovely Medua

> 'Clad in a vesture of unknowen geare
> And uncouth fashion, yet her well became,
> That seem'd like silver, sprinckled here and theare
> With glittering spangs that did like starres appeare,
> And wav'd upon, like water Chamelot,
> To hide the metall, which yet every where
> Bewrayd it selfe, to let men plainely wot
> It was no mortall worke, that seem'd and yet was not.

> Her Goodly lockes adowne her backe did flow
> Unto her waste, with flowres bescattered,
> The which ambrosiall odours forth did throw
> To all about, and all her shoulders spred
> As a new spring; and likewise on her hed
> A Chapelet of sundry flowers she wore,
> From under which the deawy humour shed
> Did tricle downe her haire, like to the hore
> Congealed litle drops which doe the morne adore.'   (*Ibid.*, 45, 46.)

The lovely Medua is more a bride than a river, and Spenser's
own bride in the *Epithalamion* is very like her.   Elizabeth
Boyle is compared to the moon and

> 'Her long loose yellow locks like golden wyre
> Sprinckled with perle, and perling flowres atweene,
> Doe lyke a golden mantle her attyre;
> And, being crowned with a girland greene,
> Seeme lyke some mayden Queene.'   (*Epithalamion,* 154–158.)

The mixture of silver and gold is the same, but Medua's shimmering robe is intended to suggest at once the play of light on the river and an ethereal, almost spiritual, quality in the physical element—

> 'to let men plainly wot
> It was no mortall worke, that seem'd and yet was not.'

The apotheosis of Spenser's bride is otherwise contrived.

Medua is attended by the fifty daughters of Nereus and with the long catalogue of names, with epithets mostly vague except for the recurring suggestion of whiteness, the picture flows into a conventional design based on memories of the sea covered with white-crested waves:

> 'White hand Eunica, proud Dynamene,
>   Joyous Thalia, goodly Amphitrite,
>   Lovely Pasithee, kinde Eulimene,
>   Lightfoote Cymothoe, and sweete Melite,
>   Fairest Pherusa, Phao lilly white,
>   Wondred Agave, Poris, and Nesaea,
>   With Erato that doth in love delite,
>   And Panopae, and wise Protomedaea,
> And snowy neckd Doris, and milkewhite Galathaea:
>   (*F.Q.* IV. xi. 49.)

> 'Fresh Alimeda deckt with girlond greene;
>   Hyponeo with salt-bedewed wrests;
>   Laomedia like the christall sheene;
>   Liagore much praisd for wise behests;
>   And Psamathe for her brode snowy brests;'   (*Ibid.*, 51.)

The names are taken with two exceptions from Hesiod's list of the Nereids, and the order suggests that he had consulted the authority directly or indirectly. He has omitted Thoe and Cymatologe, and substituted two names apparently of his own invention—Poris and 'Phao lilly white.' Few of the Nereids had clear identities in myth-ology, but Spenser's epithets here and there suggest an

etymology, and so give the association he requires.   The
names are musical chords haunted by wraiths of thought,
by emotions and meanings pressing to the gates of consciousness like the babes in the Garden of Adonis.   Thus
the name Psa(m)mathe is from the poetical word for the
sands of the sea and was used proverbially for a countless
multitude (Liddell and Scott), but Spenser's epithet 'snowy'
suggests rather the broad bosom of the sea itself.   Thoe
was perhaps omitted because he had called Proto 'swift,'
and the full sound of Poris was required in the place it
occupied.   But 'Phao lilly white' is the key-note of the
passage: it must be from Phaos, meaning light, and suggesting both life and joy, and Phao is the prototype of all
the Nereids, the embodiments of Aeschylus' 'many-
twinkling laughter of the sea.'

The allegory in the whole episode is so obvious and so
slight that we get the impression of a physical world living
its own withdrawn, uncommunicating, unintelligible life.
Nevertheless, the processional form and the flowing rhythm
in which the pageant's passing is described blends the
figures into a single stream, so that their transience is their
essential characteristic, and the transience gives an ethereal
and intellectual quality.   Flowing water always fascinated
Spenser, as it did Shelley.   A river is so perfect an image
of time that it seems scarcely metaphorical, and time as
we have seen was to him the very substance of the things
of sense.

The critics who complain that the most beautiful episodes
and figures in *The Faerie Queene* are mere irrelevant
decoration have been in the habit of pointing to the stories
of Florimell [1] and Marinell, which run through the third

[1] It has been pointed out by A. B. Gough and H. M. Belden, that the
suggestion for the true and false Florimells probably came from Euripides'
Helen, in which there is an evil phantom Helen, whose sins are imputed
to the true, confirmation of the identification being that the true Helen is

and fourth Books. Mr. Notcutt, in his Essay on the Critics of Spenser (*Essays and Studies of the English Associa- tion*, Vol. XII) has attempted to refute this sort of accusa- tion by what we may call the dramatic plea. He assumes that the figures are all at once moral qualities and attempts at representations of real men and women. He says, in particular, that Florimell is a picture of the beautiful chaste woman without discretion and that her misfortunes are the logical result of her folly. Such an interpreta- tion appears to do more wrong to Spenser than that which regards those figures as the airy creations of vacant fancy.

Florimell is in love with, and is finally united to, Marinell, which implies that they are of the same order of being: an examination of the one ought therefore to throw light on the other, and it is best to begin with Marinell, because we are not confused in his case by the introduction of moral questions in the narrower sense. He is fleetingly a type of the noble savage knight, but that is, as it were, a metaphor, for he is properly the incarnation of the poetry of the sea. Miss Sitwell's two phrases, 'those delicate paladins the waves' and 'the goat-foot satyr waves,' [1] catch as in a silver mirror two aspects of Spenser's Marinell. The sea is always to the poet a symbol of ultimate loveli- ness—or even more than a symbol—the body, as it were, of the Heavenly Beauty. There is some link between it and the Graces, those 'Maidens lily-white'—which 'deck the body and adorn the mind.' They are the grand- children of Ocean, and Jove begot them 'coming from

persecuted by Proteus, as the true Florimell is in *The Faerie Queene*. This does not, I think, invalidate the theory in the text. Helen stands for all physical loveliness, and the memory of the tale of Troy haunts the whole of Book III. But if Spenser had intended his readers to make the con- nection, he would have thrown out such gossamer links as he does in the case of Hellenore.

[1] Edith Sitwell, *Troy Park*.

fruitful glee of Thetis' wedding with Aeacidae.' The connection is a good example of the way in which the code-
key of allegory or even of symbolism fails to unlock
any but the most unimportant of Spenser's wards. The
Graces—that ethereal quintessence of lovely human behaviour—cannot be derived from the sea as a physical
phenomenon, but their essential quality can only be conveyed by the analogy of sea-foam enveloped in a moonlit
mantle of mythology.

At his first introduction Marinell's extra-human quality
is indicated by the comparison—

> 'Like as a sacred oxe that carelesse stands
>   With gilden hornes and flowry girlonds crownd,
>   Proud of his dying honor and deare bandes,
>   Whiles th'altars fume with frankincense arownd,
>   All suddeinly, with mortall stroke astownd,
>   Doth groveling fall, and with his streaming gore
>   Distaines the pillours and the holy grownd,
>   And the faire flowres that decked him afore:
> So fell proud Marinell upon the pretious shore.'
>
> (*F.Q.* III, iv, 17.)

The sacrifice has no terror in it, and suggests the sunlit
peace of Keats's *Grecian Urn*, but it flings round Marinell
as it were a mantle of consecration, making him a sort of
demi-god and yet sub-human by association with the dumb
and massive creature. Then Spenser heaps up the splen-
dours of the Pretious Strand which is

> 'bestrowed all with rich aray
>   Of pearles and pretious stones of great assay,
>   And all the gravell mixt with golden owre:' (*Ibid.*, 18.)

The terror of the sea is mingled with the glamour of this

> 'Wealth of th' East, and pompe of Persian Kings;
>   Gold, amber, Yvorie, perles, owches, rings.' (*Ibid.*, 23.)

(Milton was to remember the passage when he wrote of

> 'the wealth of Ormuz or of Inde
> Or where the gorgeous East with richest hand
> Showers on her Kings barbaric pearl and gold.')
>
> (P.L. II. 314.)

This splendour was the inheritance of Marinell, for Nereus, entreated by his daughter, Marinell's mother, had commanded

> 'his heaped waves
> Out of their hollow bosome forth to throw
> All the huge threasure, which the sea below
> Had in his greedie gulfe devoured deepe,
> And him enriched through the overthrow
> And wreckes of many wretches, which did weepe
> And often waile their wealth, which he from them did keepe.'
>
> (F.Q. III. iv. 22.)

Spenser is aiming at the same effect as Shakespeare in Clarence's account of his dream in *Richard III*:

> 'Methought I saw a thousand fearful wrecks
> Ten thousand men that fishes gnawed upon:
> Wedges of gold, great anchors, heaps of pearl
> Inestimable stones, unvalued jewels,
> All scatter'd in the bottom of the sea;
> Some lay in dead men's skulls; and in those holes
> Where eyes did once inhabit, there were crept,
> As 'twere in scorn of eyes, reflecting gems,
> Which woo'd the slimy bottom of the deep
> And mock'd the dead bones that lay scatter'd by.'
>
> (Rich. III. 1–4.)

Both poets seek to give the significance of the sea—inexhaustible treasure in a material form that has a strange magic, as of matter intensified to divinity; associated with human tears, and human helplessness before the insatiable and unfathomable waters. Shakespeare has gone on to the further thought that corruption is the generator of some kinds of beauty, and he has intensified the desolation and humiliation of the poor wrecked bodies. Spenser did not desire to introduce here the element of repulsion. Marinell and all associated with him is beautiful though touched with a delicate melancholy and always haunted by the ideas of wildness and power. The imagery grouped round him is a further extension of his personality, but much of it is too subtle for explicit interpretation. The value, for example, of such an episode as Cymoent's lamentation for her son and her journey to him with her attendant sisters, is dimly perceived when we read how Shelley's Urania comes from her Paradise to lament the dead Adonais. The passage was clearly inspired by that of Spenser, and the cloud of ethereal beings that hover round Urania and the dead Adonais are the later poet's articulation of Spenser's meaning. There is perhaps a suggestion of metaphor, which should not be pressed too far, of the stormy sea sinking back into an azure calm when the Nereids disarm Marinell, that they may search and salve his 'griesly wound' and lay him on

'Their watchet mantles frindgd with silver round.'

(*F.Q.* III. iv. 40.)

Marinell is not the sea, but the value which the sea has for the mind of man. Neptune, who represents the simple physical element, beholds the journey of the sorrowing Nereids 'Yet wist not what their wailing ment.' Marinell is associated with the marriage of the Thames and the Medway, although he is unable to feast with those simple personifications of physical phenomena, because

'he was halfe mortall, being bred
Of mortall sire, though of immortall wombe,
He might not with immortall food be fed,
Ne with th' eternall Gods to bancket come;'

(*F.Q.* IV. xii. 4.)

As all the rivers are present at the banquet one must suppose that here the eternal Gods are simply the seemingly ageless forces of the natural world, to whom Marinell is akin through his mother; while his mortal part represents his relation to the human mind.   As he wanders shut out from the joy of the physical world he hears the lamentations of the imprisoned Florimell and is stirred to pity and love of her.   Their marriage is the subject of the last canto of the Book of Friendship, coming immediately after that of the rivers in their purely physical aspect, and representing both a wider and a more spiritual harmony.

Florimell, it is clear, must belong to the same order of being as Marinell.   She was suggested, no doubt, by Ariosto's Angelica, but Angelica is a beautiful woman with not a little coquetry, and Spenser's thought of her has been purified and illuminated by a memory of the passage in Ovid's *Metamorphoses* where Daphne flies from Apollo— 'auctaque forma fuga est.'   He says nothing, as Milton does, to remind us of the passage in Ovid: [1] but the perception of the loveliness of the idea of flight, of its power like some refiner's fire, or the magic of moonlight, to add the last wonder to beauty had remained with him.   The passage in Ovid helps to prove what Spenser was attempting; a knowledge of it adds little to the picture.   Spenser has sucked all the honey from the flower.

> 'All suddenly out of the thickest bush
>   Upon a milk-white palfrey all alone
>   A goodly lady did foreby them rush,
>   Whose face did seeme as cleare as Christall stone,
>   And eke, through feare, as white as whales bone:
>   Her garments all were wrought of beaten gold,
>   And all her steed with tinsell trappings shone,
>   Which fledd so fast that nothing mote him hold,
> And scarse them leasure gave her passing to behold.'
>
> (*F.Q.* III. i. 15.)

Florimell is pure physical loveliness of white and gold, magically etherealized by the poetic alchemy of her terror-

---

[1] See *Comus*, lines 661–2.

stricken flight.   She is the incarnation of all transient
beauty of the earth:

> 'Like hues and harmonies of evening
> Like clouds in starlight widely spread
> Like memory of music fled.'

To ask why she is so unfortunate, for ever flying and for
ever caught and imprisoned by cruel creatures, is to

> 'ask why the sunlight not for ever
> Weaves rainbows o'er yon mountain river.'

But she is not what Shelley called Intellectual Beauty.
When Prince Arthur pursues her, he believes her to be
this Intellectual Beauty—his Gloriana; but he is mistaken,
and when he learns her name he agrees to help in her rescue
as part of his general knightly duty to succour the helpless,
not because she is the goal of his proper quest.   Florimell
belongs to the world of sense, but she belongs to it as
Marinell belongs to it: as he is the beauty and terror that
men perceive in the sea, so she is the ineffable sadness of
all transitory loveliness of the earth.   Her name suggesting
the honeyed breath of flowers links her as by dewy cobwebs with Proserpine, and that may have been her chief
association for the poet.[1]   As the daughter of the Earth-
Mother is carried off by Aidoneus to his dark realm among
the dead, so Florimell is carried off by Proteus to his
dwelling beneath the sea, where he importunes her to give
herself to him.   The analogy of her fate transfers to
Florimell some of the haunting pathos of the Greek maiden
goddess.   It is fitting that the strangeness and wild beauty
of the sea should be married to this maiden representative
of the pathos of the fading things of earth.

The false Florimell is an artist's symbol of beauty which
he has outgrown.   When placed beside the true beauty
it vanishes away.   It may be suggested that the tourna-
ment in honour of Florimell is Spenser's jesting portrait

[1] cf. Note on p. 78.

of his fellow-artists' struggles to capture the ideal loveliness. The girdle of Florimell, which can only be worn by a pure woman, is the magic charm of beauty which can only belong to what is true. It blends the memory of the girdle of Venus with those of the magical properties of the mediaeval romances. Chastity is here probably an emblem of aesthetic purity. The insistence on morality in a rather narrow sense as the whole of Spenser's theme has blinded us to the infinite variety of 'the waies of Faerie land.' The whole tone of this episode, and indeed of everything that concerns the false Florimell, is light and playful—she is never morally evil as Duessa-Fidessa is evil.

Marinell and Florimell are embodiments of the world of sense at the point where it is about to be transmuted into the world of soul. At the other end of the scale are the satyrs, representing crude but innocent physical existence. The poet has for those shaggy, clumsy creatures, a liking akin on the one hand to his forefathers' feeling for the grotesques of mediaeval art and on the other to Rupert Brooke's love of rough blankets (*The Great Lover*). They rescue Una from the lust of Sansloy, and although at first terrified she soon realizes their innocence and goes with them 'without suspect of harm,' while they 'as glad as birdes of joyous Prime' dance round her, shouting and sounding their merry pipes.

Satyrane, son of a satyr and a mortal woman, by whose help she finally escapes, is perhaps of the same order of being as Marinell. The story of his mother's terror when she saw him as a child playing with the lion's whelps gives to the picture of this sub-human world the combination of fierce strength and purely physical tenderness. That world not only does Una, the touchstone of goodness, no hurt, but even saves her and is in turn illuminated by her presence. But it cannot hold her: she blesses it and passes on her way.

The companion picture is that of Hellenore. Cast off by Paridell, who had seduced her from her husband Malbecco, she wanders in the woods till found by a troop of satyrs, and goes to dwell with them. We see her dancing in the forest-glades with the satyrs 'full of fresh delight,' and that picture too has the comeliness of physical health, of 'the wells of life.' But in this case Spenser spares us none of its grosser side, and Hellenore is wedded to both when she 'chose amongst the jolly satyrs still to wonne,' and a life that is for them innocent degrades the human being. Hellenore sinks into the unmoral animal world, forgetting not only Malbecco but 'eke Sir Paridell, all were he deare,' and once she has so sunk the poet leaves her without comment, which is the more remarkable because of the emphasis in the condemnation of her husband. For Malbecco, having been witness to Hellenore's full degradation and been utterly rejected by her in spite of his offered forgiveness, and having besides lost his wealth, is wasted and petrified into Jealousy incarnate and throws himself from

> 'a rockie hill
> Over the sea suspended dreadfully. . . .

> But through long anguish and self-murdring thought
> He was so wasted and forpined quight
> That all his substance was consumed to nought
> And nothing left but like an airy spright
> That on the rocks he fell so flit and light
> That he thereby received no hurt at all
> But chaunced on a craggy cliff to light;
> Whence he with crooked clawes so long did crall
> That at the last he found a cave with entrance small.

> .   .   .   .   .

> There dwels he ever, miserable swaine,
> Hateful both to himself and every wight;
> Where he through privy griefe, and horror vaine
> Is waxen so deform'd, that he has quight
> Forgot he was a man, and Gealosie is hight.'

So ends canto x, but canto xi opens with a fierce denuncia-
tion of the 'hateful hellish snake . . . fowle gealosie' and
with the emphatic conclusion 'of all the passions in the
mind thou vilest art.' Malbecco has suffered horribly,
having had complete confirmation of his wildest suspicions,
and yet it is he, rather than the wanton Hellenore, who
is so utterly condemned. To Spenser the world of sense
has, as it were, the primitive innocence of our first parents
before they had tasted of the tree of knowledge of good
and evil, and he finds in it rest and refreshment from the
arid wilderness of purely mental evil. The brilliant light
of the spiritual world involves the darkest shadow of sin.

But there is throughout the story of Hellenore, Paridell
and Malbecco something objective in the treatment. The
poet seems to think of them rather as elements in life
than as individuals to whom moral standards are relevant.
Hellenore's relation to Paridell is constantly associated
with the story of Helen and Paris. Paridell claims descent
from Paris and tells some passages from the Tale of Troy.
Hellenore is called 'the second Helen' and she lights with
her own hands a fire to consume what she has left of her
husband's wealth.

> 'for sport or for despight
> As Hellen, when she saw aloft appeare
> The Trojane flames and reach to hevens hight,
> Did clap her hands, and joyed at that dolefull sight.'
>
> (*F.Q.* III. x. 12.)

Clearly we are meant to catch the glamour of the world's
greatest story, the excitement of men's desire for matchless
beauty and the burning of the topless towers of Ilium.
Hellenore and her sins do not affect the heroes of the poem.
For them she belongs to the 'breath of outward circumstance,' to the facts among which the individual soul
moves, but which it cannot alter, facts which are the background against which the drama of the soul is played.

These consist both of physical phenomena and of secular
events.   In Marinell and Florimell and the satyrs physical
phenomena and individual elements are represented, but in
the Tale of Troy and in certain episodes which we find
chiefly in Book VI Spenser seems to be watching the
pattern of the work of temporal life—the apparently fanciful
convolutions in its movement, rather than logical and
ethical sequences.   The prevailing character of this life is
rustic, romantically wild, even savage.   His mental picture is, of course, coloured by the conditions of the Ireland
of his day, but he has generalized these particular circumstances until he sees them as an allegory of a law of life.
The story of the carrying off by brigands of Pastorella,
her foster-father and all her people, and the picture of the
robbers' cave and of their fortunes there is of this sort:

> 'Their dwelling in a little island was
>   Covered with shrubby woods, in which no way
>   Appeard for people in nor out to pas,
> Nor any footing fynde for overgrowen gras.
>
> For underneath the ground their way was made
>   Through hollow caves, that no man mote discover
>   For the thicke shrubs, which did them alwaies shade
>   From view of living wight, and covered over,
>   But darknesse dred and daily night did hover
>   Through all the inner parts, wherein they dwelt;
>   Ne lightned was with window, nor with lover,
>   But with continuall candle-light, which delt
> A doubtfull sense of things, not so well seene as felt.'
>
> <div align="right">(<i>F.Q.</i> VI. x. 41–42.)</div>

The chaffering between the brigands and slave merchants
and the quarrel that grows out of the Captain's refusal to
sell Pastorella is told with realistic ruthlessness.   The
captives are killed to prevent their assisting the weaker
side, and the quintessence of the physical horrors of the
night is given in a few lines, which show that Spenser

could condense when it was his hint to do so. Substance here has melted into grim shadow, and abstraction and generalization combine to suggest horrible chaos:

> 'And the mad steele about doth fiercely fly,
> Not sparing wight, ne leaving any balke
> But making way for death at large to walke;
> Who in the horror of the griesly night,
> In thousand dreadful shapes doth mongst them stalke
> And makes huge havocke, whiles the candlelight
> Out quenched, leaves no skill nor difference of wight.' (*Ibid.*, xi. 16.)

The detail of the quenched candle affords a point from which the darkness becomes visible and vacancy is filled with shadows.

The episode of the attempted sacrifice of Serena by the cannibals is the climax of this sort of effect—of the attempt to depict this wild brutality at the heart of life, which yet has a strange beauty. The savage appetites of the cannibals, the fierce fanaticism of the Priest who is to sacrifice her, the detailed description of her beauty when her clothes have been torn off her, the barbarous noises— bagpipes and horns that 'shrill' and 'shriek' aloud, and human cries that 'did the ayre with terror fill'—all these are an expression of this fundamental quality in secular existence. But as in the case above, the crude horrors are blended for the rescuer Calepine, by the uncertain gleams of light into a picture in which the vivid details lacking connections have acquired a new value:

> 'There by th'uncertaine glims of starry night,
> And by the twinkling of their sacred fire,
> He mote perceive a little dawning sight
> Of all, which there was doing in that quire:
> Mongst whom a woman spoyld of all attire
> He spyde lamenting her unluckie strife,
> And groning sore from grieved hart entire
> Eftsoones he saw one with a naked knife
> Readie to launch her brest, and let out loved life.' (*Ibid.*, viii. 48.)

The details are all points of eerie light—star beams, sparkles of the sacrificial fire, glimpses of the woman's white body, gleams of the brandished knife—which thus becomes the stuff of the picture. The horrible story is sublimated into vaporous beauty. It is a good illustration of the way in which crude substance forgets itself to moonlight under Spenser's touch.

The same power of transfiguring intensely sensuous material is shown in his treatment of the Venus and Adonis myth. Spenser twice paints a picture of the lovers, and it has been thought that Shakespeare's poem was suggested by the first of these—the description in Book III, canto i, of a tapestry in Castle Joyous. Milton was clearly thinking of the passage in the sixth canto of the same book, when he wrote the last speech of the spirit in *Comus*.

Castle Joyous is a Venusberg, the kingdom of Lust, and it is Spenser's business to stresst he element of sensuous desire, which the arras on its walls depicts. It is, then, characteristic of him, that here where the baser import of the story *must* be shown, he does not represent the persons as alive, but embalmed—enchanted as it were into the stillness of a tapestry design. The description begins and ends with the turning of Adonis into a flower, a repetition which gives the effect of a completed pattern while the generalized description of how Venus 'entyst the boy,' and the garlands of flowers with which she crowns him remind us of the flourishes in such a tapestry picture.

Shakespeare's Venus, on the other hand, is all too much a living, wanton woman; his Adonis is a sulky boy. The world which frames them is as feelingly alive as they. Shakespeare has added the horse and the palfrey, poor Wat and the whole natural background of wood and hill, and the process of day and night. He has stressed Adonis' reluctance and developed in great detail the description of Venus. She describes herself:

'Thou canst not see one wrinkle on my brow,
Mine eyes are grey, and bright and quick in turning;
My flesh is soft and plumpe.'

She dances on the sands 'like a nymph with long dishevelled hair.' Whether we like it or not, Shakespeare's characteristic faculty is here—the faculty of making living, audible, tangible men and women stand before us, so that we feel their breath upon our faces. Shakespeare's Venus has no mantle, it is her flesh we are to feel: Spenser's has 'a mantle, colour'd like the starry skyes' which she spreads over Adonis as he lies asleep 'and her soft arms lay underneath his hed,' so that we think of the goddess as the incarnation of a summer midnight beautiful and tender to man's weakness.

More congenial to Spenser's basic philosophy is the mystical aspect of Adonis which is developed in the sixth canto. There the Garden of Adonis is certainly not evil: in it the fair and virtuous Amoret is fostered and 'trained in true feminitie'; and there we are told, some say Adonis yet lies in secret 'lapp'd in flowers and precious spicerye.

'There now he lives in everlasting joy,
    With many of the gods in company
    Which thither haunt, and with the winged boy
    Sporting himselfe in safe felicity.'   (*F.Q.* III. vi. 49.)

The poet goes on to link Adonis with the beautiful late myth of Cupid and Psyche, with all that it implies of spiritual discipline and loveliness; Cupid dwells in the garden with

'Fayre Psyche to him lately reconcild,
After long troubles and unmeet upbrayes.

        .   .   .   .   .

But now in stedfast love and happy state
She with him lives, and hath him borne a chyld
Pleasure.'

The passage, as Warton noticed long ago, inspired the

lovely speech of the spirit at the close of Milton's *Comus*.
We have the same superficially arbitrary juxtaposition of
the Adonis story with that of Cupid and Psyche, and Milton's passage, a-quiver with memories of beauty, is more
explicit than Spenser's and reflects back light on his great
'original.'

Already in the *Nativity Ode*, Milton had shown a consciousness of deeper meaning in the Adonis story, for there
Adonis appears as 'the wounded Thammuz' whom the
Tyrian maidens mourn, and Thammuz is a form of Osiris,
the dying god. This mystic interpretation is, I think,
caught from Spenser as the artistic method certainly is.
Both poets proceed by grouping together figures and
incidents from widely separated contexts, so that they cast
coloured shadows and modify each other. Milton sets
Adonis in

> 'the gardens fair
> Of Hesperus and his daughters three
> That sing about the golden tree.'   (*Comus*, 981–3.)

There

> 'young Adonis oft reposes
> Waxing well of his deep wound
> In slumber soft, and on the ground
> Sadly sits the Assyrian Queen:
> But far above in spangled sheen
> Celestial Cupid, her fam'd son, advanc'd
> Holds his dear Psyche sweet entranc'd
> After her wandring labours long
> Till free consent the gods among
> Make her his eternal bride,
> And from her fair unspotted side
> Two blissful twins are to be born,
> Youth and Joy.'   (*Ibid.*, 999–1011.)

The ladies of the Hesperides haunt many of Milton's
loveliest passages. They come no doubt originally from

the marvellous chorus in the *Hippolytus* with its longing to
fly away and be at rest in

> 'The land of the daughters of the sunset
> The apple-trees, the singing and the gold.'

But I suspect that they are touched by the memory of the
three Graces who dance beside a tree laden with golden
apples in Botticelli's Primavera.   He had almost certainly
remembered it when he wrote in *L'Allegro* of

> 'Zephyr with Aurora playing
> When he met her once a-maying.'

Two other notes sound rather more faintly.   Milton's
great poetic hero was at first to be King Arthur, and
Paradise Lost and *Paradise Regained* are nowhere more
magnificent than when the treasures that had been gathered
for the earlier theme are spilt in some passing allusion.
He was deeply read in all the literature of romance and
can hardly have forgotten Malory's record of King Arthur's
words to Sir Bedevere, 'I will unto the vale of Avilion
for to hele me of my grievous wounde,' nor the legend
that he was not dead but living in Faerie, even as Adonis
lives in the Hesperian gardens 'waxing well of his deep
wound.'

The other note is introduced by calling Venus the Assyrian
Queen.   Eighteenth-century critics wished to change it to
the 'Cyprian Queen,' but there is no authority for this
version.   One remembers that 'the wounded Thammuz'
is linked with 'the mooned Ashtaroth, Heavens Queen
and Mother both,' and there is little doubt that Milton
here wished to associate Venus rather with the strangeness
of Asiatic half-barbarous belief than with the simple loveliness of Greek or Latin myth.   Again, the lastl ines of
Comus suggest a connection, corroborated by other details,
between Milton's poem and Ben Jonson's Masque *Pleasure*

reconciled to Virtue.   Mercury calls to the Masquers to
return to their mountain top and the pursuit of Virtue who

> 'though a stranger here on earth
> In heaven she hath her right of birth.
>
> There, there is Virtue's seat
> Strive to keep her your own
> 'Tis only she can make you great
> Though place here make you known.'

Milton's spirit calls from the

> 'broad fields of the sky
> Mortals that would follow me
> Love virtue, she alone is free
> She can teach you how to clime
> Higher than the sphery chime
> Or if Virtue feeble were
> Heaven itself would stoop to her.'

The spirit with his 'sky-robes spun out of Iris' woof' is
something of an angel—God's messenger as Mercury is
Jove's; but he has memories of Ariel, and the Heaven
from which he comes and to which he calls is a spiritual
Paradise on earth.   We may compare the passage in
Paradise Lost (Book III. ii. 460–62) when the poet, denying
the hypothesis that the moon is the place of the Paradise
of Fools, goes on:

> 'Those argent fields more likely habitants,
> Translated saints, or *middle spirits, hold*
> *Betwixt the angelical and human kind.*'

That this is his nature and such his dwelling is clearer
in the original form of the opening speech in *Comus* as
given in the Trinity College manuscript.   It is there certain
that he is describing, not the Christian Heaven of the holy
dead, but rather an Elysium where dwell beautiful spirits
who belong to another order of being, and are therefore
not within the precincts of Heaven.

'Before the starry threshold of Jove's court
My mansion is, where those immortal shapes
Of bright aerial spirits live inspher'd
In regions mild of calm and serene air
Amidst the Hesperian gardens, on whose banks
Bedew'd with nectar and celestial songs
Eternal roses grow and hyacinth
And fruits of golden rind, on whose fair tree
The scaly-harness'd dragon ever keeps
His unenchanted eye: around the verge
And sacred limits of this blissful isle
The jealous ocean, that old river, winds
His far extended arms, till with steep fall
Half his waste flood the wild Atlantic fills
And half the slow unfathom'd Stygian pool.
I doubt me, gentle mortals, these may seem
Strange distances to hear, and unknown climes.'

In the final version the isle, round which the river Ocean
winds, was Britain, but here it is clearly a Paradise closely
parallel to Spenser's Gardens of Adonis, and the 'immortal
shapes' who dwell in those 'regions mild of calm and serene
air' recall at once the virtuous Pagans born before Christ in
Dante's Elysium and the famous friends and lovers whom
Sir Scudamour saw when he went to win Amoret. Of this
demesne the love-story of Venus and Adonis and the mystical
wounding and healing of Adonis is the centre. To Spenser
as apparently to his 'son' Milton, the Venus and Adonis
myth was not merely an expression, as it was to Shakespeare,
of the relations between the sexes. To Spenser Adonis
stands for the mystery of the sensible world, for its loveliness and terror, and its law of life through suffering and
death. Amoret and his own bride belong to Adonis'
realm, for there is one further identification that we must
make. In Book VI Calidore

'Chaunst to come, far from all peoples troad
Unto a place whose pleasaunce did appere

> To passe all others on the earth which were:
> For all that ever was by natures skill
> Devized to worke delight was gathered there,
> And there by her were poured forth at fill.'

This lovely spot—Mount Acidale—is guarded by trees

> 'Which did all winter as in summer bud,
> Spredding pavilions for the birds to bower.'

A 'silver flud' runs round the mount and

> 'Nymphs and Faeries by the bancks did sit
> In the woods shade, which did the waters crowne,
> Keeping all noysome things away from it,
> And to the waters fall tuning their accents fit.'   (*F.Q.* VI. x. 7.)

That last line 'echoes' not only the singing in the Garden of Adonis but the refrain in the *Epithalamion*. To this 'pleasaunce' Venus used to resort

> 'there to repose
> And rest herselfe, as in a gladsome port
> Or with the Graces there to play and sport.'
>
> (*Ibid.*, 9.)

And here Calidore sees the vision of the hundred lily maidens dancing in a ring.

> 'but in the midst of them
> Three other ladies did both daunce and sing,
> The whilst the rest them round about did hemme
> And like a girlond did in compasse stemme:
> And in the midst of those same three, was placed
> Another Damzell, as a precious gemme,
> Amidst a ring most richly well enchaced.'   (*Ibid.*, 12.)

This damzell is 'crownd with a rare girlond'

> 'and ever, as the crew
> About her daunst, sweet flowres, that far did smell
> And fragrant odours they uppon her threw;
> But most of all, those three did her with gifts endew.'
>
> (*Ibid.*, 14.)

The three are 'the Graces, daughters of delight.'

> 'but that faire one
> That in the midst was placed paramount
> Was she to whom that shepheard pypt alone,
> That made him pipe so merrily, as never none.   (*Ibid.*, 15.)
>
> She was to weete that jolly shepheards lasse,'   (*Ibid.*, 16.)

the poet's own lady of the *Amoretti* and *Epithalamion*, who, as the poet repeats again, 'made (him) often pipe and now to pipe apace.' The vanishing of the vision at Sir Calidore's approach, Colin's distress and breaking of his pipe, with his explanations to Calidore make it clear that the lily maidens are a symbol for the poetic experience:

> 'Not I so happy, answer'd then that swaine,
> As thou unhappy, which them thence didst chace,
> Whom by no means thou canst recall againe,
> For being gone, none can them bring in place
> But whom they of themselves list so to grace.'   (*Ibid.*, 20.)

It is poetry inspired by his lady, and definitely of an humbler strain than that in which he sings great Gloriana, but he claims that it should not be forgotten:

> 'Great Gloriana, greatest Majesty
> Pardon thy shepheard, mongst so many layes
> As he hath sung of thee in all his dayes,
> To make one minime of thy poore handmayd,
> And underneath thy foote to place her prayse,
> That when thy glory shall be farre displayd
> To future age of her this mention may be made.'   (*Ibid.*, 28.)

It is pastoral poetry, the poetry of the sensible world, and of his bride who was its crown and symbol. Spenser's successors usually call him Colin Clout, as if in mind of this prayer for commemoration of his human love, but the poetry which enshrines it, though a necessary preparation, was not the task to which he felt himself called.

CHAPTER V

The Love Theme

Dean Church's fundamental dislike of Spenser's genius
manifests itself in his vehement attack on the prominence
of the love theme in *The Faerie Queene*. 'All Spenser's
virtues,' he writes approvingly, 'spring from a root of
manliness . . . (*but*) they have with him another condition
as universal. They all grow and are nourished from the
soil of love; the love of beauty, the love and service of
fair women. . . . Spenser's types of manhood are imper-
fect without the idea of an absorbing and overmastering
passion of love. . . . In one shape or another it meets
us at every turn; it is never absent; it is the motive and
stimulant of the whole activity of the poem. The picture
of life held up before us is the literal rendering of Coleridge's
lines:

> "All thoughts, all passions, all delights,
> Whatever stirs this mortal frame
> All are but ministers of love
> And feed his sacred flame." '

'We still think with Spenser,' he goes on, 'about the
paramount place of manliness, as the foundation of all
worth in human character. We have ceased to think with
him about the rightful supremacy of love, even in the
imaginative conception of human life. . . . A world of
which (love) is the law is not even in fiction a world which
we can conceive possible, or with which experience enables
us to sympathize. It is, of course, a purely artificial and
conventional reading of the facts of human life.'

Now many thinkers of the present day would be prepared to say that the view which Church here represents as that of Spenser—the view that sexual love is the mainspring of life—is a true picture of the facts. But Church has failed to see that for Spenser the word covers a vast system of relations and a scale of emotions in which sexual love is only one note, and that the anthropomorphic nature of the imagery is to some extent accountable for the dominance of the love theme. The marriage of the Thames and the Medway is an example of the 'sustaining love' woven through the web of physical and inanimate being. The many knights who pursue Florimell are inspired by an aesthetic passion for sensuous beauty, here merely personified in a woman, as Prince Arthur's quest of Gloriana is the symbol of the soul's pursuit of the supreme good.

Love is, in fact, Spenser's symbol for the unifying and dynamic forces in existence. As indicated above, when dealing with the physical universe, he accepts it as the creative aspect of that universe, and therefore good; but in the purely human relations, except when love is a symbol of the spiritual aspiration, the poet prefers friendship. The third and fourth Books are very closely linked together and, though it is probable that the fourth Book has been somehow disturbed or rearranged, it still remains clear that it was originally planned as an integral part of the third, and the culmination of its argument. The fourth Book is a celebration of friendship, the third was an analysis of sexual love, and Spenser states explicitly that friendship is greater than love.

> 'Hard is the doubt, and difficult to deeme,
>   When all three kinds of love together meet,
>   And doe dispart the hart with powre extreme,
>   Whether shall weigh the balance downe; to weet
>   The dear affection unto kindred sweet,

Or raging fire of love to womankind,
Or zeale of friends combynd with virtues meet.
But of them all the bond of virtuous mind
Meseemes the gentle hart should most assured bind.

For naturall affection soone doth cease,
    And quenched is with Cupids greater flame:
    But faithful friendship doth them both suppresse,
    And them with maystring discipline doth tame,
    Through thoughts aspyring to eternall fame,
    For as the soule doth rule the earthly masse,
    And all the service of the bodie frame,
    So love of soule doth love of bodie passe,
No lesse than perfect gold surmounts the meanest brasse.'

(*F.Q.* IV. ix. 1, 2.)

The story which leads up to this pronouncement is not
very attractive, and the sentiment was common enough in
late mediaeval and early Tudor times. The Romance of
Amis and Amiloun, which it resembles, and the dramatists'
treatment of stories like those of Damon and Pythias, and
of Palamon and Arcite show how easily friendship rather
than love might have become the emotional mainspring of
modern European literature. The tendency explains why
an Elizabethan audience before 1590 might accept the
dénouement of *The Two Gentlemen of Verona*. The fundamental theme of that play is not that of love but of a
beautiful friendship between two young men, the treacherous
lapse of one under the temptation of the rival emotion and
the reinstatement of the relation after repentance and forgiveness. In all the plays written before 1600 friendship
between men is more important than has been generally
recognized.

But in fact the Book of Friendship shows that whatever
Spenser's conscious logic might conclude, in the mediaeval
theme of friendship between men he found little poetic
material. He links it closely with the Book of Love, and

makes the last three cantos tell of the winning of Amoret,
the marriage of the Thames and the Medway, and of
Marinell and Florimell. That is to say, the Book of
Friendship is really mainly concerned with marriage. It
is noticeable that the titular heroes of the book—Cambell
and Triamond—are linked by the marriage of Cambell
to Triamond's sister Cambina, and the poet concludes:

> 'So all alike did love, and loved were
> That since their days such lovers were not found elsewhere.'
>
> (*Ibid.*, iii. 52.)

On the other hand, in the very Garden of Adonis,
where Amoret is fostered, we find as a culmination of the
groups of lovers famous pairs of friends:

> 'But farre away from these, another sort
> Of lovers lincked in true harts consent,
> Which loved not as these, for like intent
> But on chaste virtue grounded their desire
> Farre from all fraud, or fayned blandishment
> Which in their spirits kindling jealous fire
> Brave thoughts and noble deeds did evermore inspire.'
>
> (*Ibid.*, x. 24.)

Such, we are told, were Hercules and Hylas, Jonathan and
David, Pylades and Orestes:

> 'All these and all that ever had been tyde
> In bands of friendship, there did live for ever.' (*Ibid.*, 27.)

Clearly Spenser wished to show that the emotion of married
love, as he conceived it, was indistinguishable from that of
exalted friendship. Moreover, Spenser's 'general end' was
'to fashion a gentleman or noble person in virtuous and
gentle discipline.' The force of the word 'fashion' has
been a little overlooked. Spenser goes on to say that some
'had rather have good *discipline* delivered plainly in way of
precepts, or sermoned at large, as they use, than thus
clowdily enwrapped in Allegoricall devises.' The 'fashion-

ing' is not so much the definition of the ideal knight as the producing in the reader of a certain state of mind. Spenser desired to discipline the emotions and imagination, very much as Dante had done in the *Divine Comedy*, till finally his own soul and that of his reader should be enriched, purified and inspired to see the vision of the perfect Beauty. Of that final vision and of the vital flame which it inspires, the word love and the emotion as we experience it in the lower reaches of existence is merely a pale reflection. That vision he would have attempted to express in his last Book, but in the earlier and particularly in the third and fourth Books the symbol must be analysed and the contemporary experience of it disciplined to the finest and richest quality of which it was capable.

The Reformation on the one hand, and the ardent rediscovery of classical literature on the other, had left the emotional world of the Elizabethans in chaos. The age tended to associate poetic value with illicit love. The ordinary marriage of the time savoured a good deal of a business alliance. The great mediaeval love-stories—Tristram and Iseult, Lancelot and Guinevere, glorified what Ascham denounced as 'bold bawdrie.' The element of some sort of a moral bar linked these with the more or less true love-stories of Heloise and Abelard and of Petrarch and Laura, and it was this last story which begot directly one of the chief poetic forms of expression of the fourteenth century—the love-sonnet sequence.

The story implied in Sidney's very beautiful *Astrophel and Stella* is typical. It is very closely modelled on Petrarch, but it may very likely be true to the facts of Sidney's own experience. The authors of literary imitations seem to have followed the methods of their contemporaries writing in the classical tongues. A situation as near as possible to that which the borrower wished to describe was selected, and the phrasing of the pattern was adapted. However that may be, contemporaries certainly accepted the outline of Astrophel's situation as the quintessence of romance. The poet is in love with a married woman, expresses his passion, tries to seduce her, but is, though his love is returned, rejected, and for a moment we have the note of ardent abstinence and exaltation. The sequence, with this climax, seems to have circulated at the time, but there are two subsequent sonnets which clearly belong to it and which speak rather of bitter disillusion:

> 'Desire, Desire, I have too dearly bought
> With price of mangled mind thy worthless ware.'

and

> 'Leave me, O Love, which reachest but to dust.'

Shakespeare's famous sonnet, which according to Sir Denys Bray's theory ended his sequence, shows a similar disgust:

> 'Th' expense of spirit in a waste of shame
> Is lust in action.'

The true Elizabethan sonnet sequence indeed, with the exception of Spenser's, betrays a conviction founded on experience, that the passion corrupts and despoils the soul. It seems to have been Spenser's intention in the *Amoretti* and *Epithalamion* to celebrate an earthly passion which was beautiful for all its physical root, and culminated in a marriage that brought to the lovers the complete realization of their highest temporal natures. It has been questioned of late years whether the *Amoretti* were all addressed to Elizabeth Boyle, whom the poet married. Much has also been made of the fact that the last three speak of a separation between the lovers and that the preceding—the eighty-fourth—curses a

> 'venomous tongue. . . .
> That with false forged lyes that thou didst tell
> In my true love did stirre up coles of fire.'

It is likely enough that some were originally written to some other woman, as a mere exercise, but it seems certain that they were arranged by the poet as they now stand to relate his greatest love-story. The 'venomous tongue' sonnet suggests indeed that the slanderer had failed, while the separation of which the last sonnets speak is that of the body, not of the heart. He compares himself to the 'culver on the bared bough' who moans for

> 'the absence of her mate
> And in her songs sends many a wishfull vow
> For his return that seems to linger late.'   (*Sonnet* lxxxix.)

He complains how slowly move the days and nights

> 'Thus I the time with expectation spend
> And faine my griefe with chaunges to beguile
> That further seems his terme still to extend
> And maketh every minute seeme a myle.'
>
> (*Sonnet* lxxxvii.)

This clearly implies that the lover is waiting and looking forward to a fixed date when his lady will return to him. The natural interpretation is that the lovers were separated for a short interval before their marriage.

We may return then to the older view that the *Amoretti* lead up to and are completed by the *Epithalamion* and that the whole sequence as it now stands was intended as the record of a virtuous passion crowned by a beautiful marriage. Now the title *Amoretti* and the fact that Amoret is the type of married chastity suggests a connection between the story told in the sonnets and the *Epithalamion* on the one hand and that of Amoret on the other. Amoret's love story begins in the eleventh canto of Book III, when Britomart finds Sir Scudamour in despair because he cannot pass the fire and enter the castle where Busyrane keeps her imprisoned. The account of her imprisonment and torture, Britomart's night in the castle and rescue of Amoret fills the twelfth canto and forms the culminating

adventure of the knight of Chastity. The earlier part of
Amoret's story—the winning of her by Sir Scudamour—
is told subsequently in Book IV, by Scudamour himself.
The tale fills a whole canto and gives a curious prominence
to Scudamour. There has been some discussion of the
meaning of Amoret's experience, but there can, I think,
be little doubt. Her tortures at the hands of Busyrane
in the House of Cupid represent the mental sufferings of
the young wife in consequence of the too lustful element
in Sir Scudamour's passion for her. This lustful element
at once wounds and inflames her. Busyrane is simply
this side of Sir Scudamour himself. This is elucidated
by the sonnets. In sonnet lxxii the poet records how the
loveliness of the too-much loved earth, and chiefly his
lady's physical beauty chain him to the ground:

> 'Oft when my spirit doth spred her bolder winges
> In mind to mount up to the purest sky
> It down is weighed with thought of earthly things
> And clogd with burden of mortality.
> Where when that soverayne beauty it doth spy
> Resembling heavens glory in her light,
> Drawne with sweet pleasures bayt, it back doth fly,
> And unto heaven forgets her former flight.'   (*Sonnet* lxxii.)

But that this attitude pains his lady he is aware, and in
sonnet lxxxiii he cries:

> 'Let not one sparke of filthy lustfull fyre
> Breake out, that may her sacred peace molest;
> Ne one light glance of sensuall desyre
> Attempt to work her gentle mindes unrest:
> But pure affections bred in spotlesse brest,'

In *The Faerie Queene* the 'lustfull fyre'

> 'A flaming fire, ymixt with smouldry smoke
> And stinking sulphur.'   (*F.Q.* III. xi. 21.)

bars Sir Scudamour's entrance into the castle. The flame
is kindled by his evil self, and prevents his pure love's

access to the lady. On the other hand, Busyrane must not be slain or Amoret will never be free: that is, passion must not be destroyed but its effect purified.

Sir Scudamour explains later that the vile enchaunter Busyrane had captured Amoret at the bridal feast, 'whilst every man surcharg'd with wine, were hedeless and ill-headed.' Even contemporaries were aware of the brutal-izing effects of the marriage entertainments of those days. Beautiful as is the ending of the love-story in the first edition of Book III, Spenser must have felt it an inadequate culmination of so fundamental a part of his thought. We require a full description of the passion in its lovely aspect to balance the masque of Cupid, and it must carry con-viction of a true experience at once vivid and complex. This consummation is given in the *Epithalamion*, the poem in which Spenser unlocked his heart.

> 'Ye learned sisters which have oftentimes
> Been to me ayding, others to adorne,
>
> .   .   .   .   .
>
> Helpe me mine owne loves prayses to resound;
> Ne let the same of any be envide:
> So Orpheus did for his owne bride!
> So I unto my selfe alone will sing,
> The woods shall to me answer, and my Eccho ring.'

The *Epithalamion*, as has been said, balances the Masque of Cupid and is very near it in form, for it is an Ode, a song to be sung by a large band of people moving in a processional dance. The English Masque appears to be a development of something of the sort, and Spenser him-self uses the word in this sense. In the simplest form a large number of people variously disguised came in pro-cession to a great person—in classical odes to the shrine of a god—paid their court and then departed in procession as they came. The balanced form and the movement seem to be the two essentials, and the combination had

always had for Spenser a mystic significance. The *Epithalamion* is very carefully constructed on this model. There
is the introduction or invocation followed by ten stanzas
while the procession gathers and leads the bride to church.
Two stanzas are allotted to the central ceremony, and then
ten stanzas bring the bride home and to the bridal chamber.
The lovely simplicity of the dedication balances the invocation and rounds it off:

> 'Song! made in lieu of many ornaments,
> With which my love should duly have been dect,
> Which cutting off through hasty accidents,
> Ye would not stay your dew time to expect,
> But promist both to recompens;
> Be unto her a goodly ornament,
> And for short time an endlesse moniment.'

The force of some of the stanzas only becomes clear when
placed beside the corresponding movement in the other
part. In the first half, nymphs strew the ground with
flowers before the bride's tender feet; in the corresponding
stanza of the second part 'young men of the town' ring
the joy-bells. The shrill, clear music of the minstrels and
the 'strong, confused noyse' of the human children crying
'Hymen, io Hymen' is balanced by silence and 'sacred
peace' and the 'winged loves' fluttering about the wedded
pair. The whole of the first part is illuminated by the sun,
while in the second the pageant of the sun is replaced by
that of the moon led on by the evening star. The bride
herself in the first part is subtly identified with the sun by
a characteristic method.

> 'Loe! where she comes along with portly pace,
> Lyke Phoebe, from her chamber of the East,
> Arysing forth to run her mighty race.'

We are intended to remember the great passage in the
Psalm, where the sun 'cometh forth as a bridegroom out

of his chamber, and rejoiceth like a mightie man to run his race.'[1] The strength, the creative masculine glory of the sun are transferred to the bride by the use of the name Phoebe, suggesting Phoebus Apollo, and the use of the Biblical reminiscence of a passage about the sun. In the corresponding stanza of the second part, the moon appears under the name of Cynthia, and is implored to remember her love for Endymion and to see herself in the bride.

The problem Spenser had set himself was not an easy one. The epithalamia of the sixteenth and seventeenth centuries are usually frankly sensuous, even sensual and licentious. They are generally addressed to the bride-groom. Spenser wished to give full expression to every aspect of the marriage, and in particular to irradiate the physical relation so that it should in no way 'work her gentle mindes unrest' to whom it was presented. To effect this he takes the Song of Solomon as the basis of his pattern. He probably accepted the contemporary inter-pretation of it as Christ's wooing of his bride the Church. In any case the reader is intended to make the analogy. The language of the Song is suggested in the description of the physical beauty of the bride, and the allegorical associations of its phrases at once purify the sensuous images and make the account of her physical loveliness flow more easily into that of 'the inward beauty of her lovely spright.'

> 'Tell me ye merchant daughters did ye see
> So fayre a creature in your towne befor,
> So sweet, so lovely, and so mild as she
> Adornd with beautyes grace and virtues store,
> Her goodly eyes like Saphyres shining bright,
> Her forehead yvory white,
> Her cheekes lyke apples which the sun hath rudded,
> Her lips like cherryes charming men to byte,

---

[1] Psalm xix. 5, Genevan version.

> Her brest like to a bowle of creame uncrudded,
> Her paps lyke lyllies budded,
> Her snowie necke lyke to a marble towre;
> And all her body like a pallace fayre,
> Ascending up, with many a stately stayre,
> To honors seat and chastities sweet bowre.'

This association of her with the Bride of Christ the Church reaches its climax in the two central stanzas, where with the triumphant lines

> 'Open the temple gates unto my love;
> Open them wide that she may enter in.'

we are reminded of the Psalmist's cry, 'Lift up your heads, O ye gates! and be ye lifted up, ye everlasting doors, and the King of Glory shall come in.' It is a parallel image to the transference to the bride under the name of Phoebe of the qualities of Phoebus Apollo. For a moment Elizabeth Boyle is 'a thing enskyed and sainted.'

But the second part of the ode links this spiritual exaltation with the mysteries of physical life. Through it there runs an undercurrent of primitive emotions, half-savage, eerie, of 'evil sprights,' witches, hobgoblins and the night raven. These things stir about the roots of life, and help to bring in from ancestral memories the sense of awe. That is the meaning of Spenser's myth that Jove lying with Night 'begot Majesty.' (*Epith.*, 331).

Sir Scudamour's story of the winning of Amoret may have been originally an independent poem. It fills, as was said, a whole canto. It may have been one of the 'Dreams' mentioned in the correspondence with Harvey, for it belongs clearly to those poems in the dream convention, which were so popular in the Middle Ages and are ultimately traceable to the *Roman de la Rose*. The whole account of Sir Scudamour's adventure, the garden, the gate of Good Desert, the figures of Daunger, Shamefastnes, Womanhood and the rest, can be paralleled in

these dream poems.   The form had become desiccated—
like a withered leaf—long before Spenser's day, but at an
earlier stage it had been the medium for the expression of
what was most 'fleshly' in mediaeval love, and the predecessor of the Venus and Adonis type of poem in Elizabethan times.   Spenser's poem, though it follows exactly
the lines of such an allegory as the Court of Love in the
Chaucer Apocrypha, has recaptured some of the tenderness of tone of the type at its best.   The young knight is
at once gallant and overawed: when he sees Amoret sitting
in the lap of Womanhood,—his

> 'hart gan throb
> And wade, in doubt, what best were to be doune:
> For sacrilege me seem'd the Church to rob
> And folly seem'd to leave the thing undoune,
> Which with so strong attempt I had begonne.
> Tho shaking off all doubt and shamefast feare
> Which ladies love I heard had never wonne
> Mongst men of worth; I to her stepped neare,
> And by the lilly hand her labour'd up to reare.'   (*F.Q.* IV. x. 53.)

And while Amoret's reluctance is clearly sincere, yet the
dawning of her love for the gentle conqueror takes away
all sense of violence.   It is a picture of natural passion
purged of all grossness.   It is a glorification of young
love without any suggestion of Platonic symbolism, and
culminating in marriage, but it does combine the ardour
of human love with the exalted note of sacred and impersonal joy.

Spenser's love philosophy is indeed quite definitely
inconsistent with the pure doctrine of Platonism.   He
had clearly found Plato's theory of human love unsatisfying.
In the absence of his lady he may 'sustayne (his) love-
affamished hart with her idea.'

> 'But with such brightnesse whylest I fill my mind,
> I starve my body, and mine eyes doe blynd.'   (*Sonnet* lxxxviii.)

To the true Platonist the Idea should be more than the bodily presence, but the poet goes on to declare:

> 'Ne joy of ought that under heaven doth hove,
> Can comfort me, but her owne joyous sight.'
>
> (*Sonnet* lxxxix.)

As Professor Renwick has pointed out, the true Platonist passes from the love of a particular woman's bodily beauty, to the idea of that beauty in her absence, and thence without looking back to the love of the universal beauty. This universal beauty is the heavenly beauty, and love of it is, according to Platonic doctrine, heavenly love. But in his *Hymns* Spenser does not ascend this ladder. Indeed, the first two Hymns really deal with Heavenly Love and Heavenly Beauty in the Platonic sense. There was an interval of time apparently between the writing of these two and of the last two, and there is a change both in tone and in form. The first two are secular, metaphysical Hymns in honour of love and beauty, but the Hymn to Heavenly Love is Christian in tone, deals with the love of God, recounts the creation and fall of the angels, the creation and fall of man, and finally the incarnation and death of the Son of God. It is thus narrative in form and gives in fact the substance of *Paradise Lost*. And the Heavenly Love in this poem is God's love to that which he has created, not man's to that which is above him. It is Agape, not Eros. Renwick thinks that Spenser then from the mere desire for structural balance wished to add a fourth Hymn to Heavenly Beauty. But Heavenly Beauty must be the object of Heavenly Love, and Heavenly Love had been depicted as divine compassion for that which was beneath it, and owed its being to it. 'Difficulty and confusion,' writes Professor Renwick, 'are evident throughout the poem, and the final vision of Sapience,' which is the object here of Heavenly Love and which, as he points out, Spenser must have found in Ficino identified with

heavenly beauty, 'captured at one bound without philosophic process . . . is isolated and in so far suspect.   There
is no hint of it in Spenser's other poems.'

But the difficulty is at least partly due to the insistence
on the Platonic doctrine.   Spenser never intended to
ascend the ladder, if such ascent involved turning his back
on that by which he did ascend.   He will not relinquish
any particle of the wealth of existence.   As he distils the
idea from a classical story to add an emotional quality to
the episode or figure he is treating, so he ranges through
the world of philosophical as well as of theological thought,
that he may with all these rainbow colours paint the 'white
radiance of Eternity.'   The four *Hymns* together form
one poem celebrating the highest beauty and its comple-
mentary emotion.   Each Hymn gives a facet of the subject, as the different figures or groups in the various masques
give facets of the subjects they represent.   He places
Eros and Agape side by side, as he had made Amoret
and Belphoebe twin-sisters, and as he in several places
had claimed the right to celebrate his own love without
irreverence to the higher loveliness of Gloriana.

> 'Sunne of the world, great glory of the sky
> That all the earth (doth) lighten with (her) rayes,'
>
> (*F.Q.* VI. x. 28.)

But his own bride he invokes as 'Divine resemblance, beauty
soveraine rare' and

> 'So farre as doth the daughter of the day
> All other lesser lights in light excell,
> So farre doth she in beautiful array
> Above all other lasses beare the bell.'   (*Ibid.*, 26.)

The 'daughter of the day' here clearly means the sun and
is a parallel to the use of the name Phoebe to identify his
bride with the sun.   Gloriana *is* the sun of the true world,
but his lady is the reflection of her in the world of
sense.

The association of the Faerie Queene with Elizabeth in
this connection is very unfortunate for the modern reader.
She is properly Glory or the Heavenly Beauty. There
can be no doubt that here—as elsewhere—Spenser does
refer to Elizabeth, and begs for pardon for daring to write
in honour of his own love when he might be spending
all his gifts in celebrating the Queen. But our failure to
sympathize with the emotional elements in Spenser's
consciousness blinds us to the comparative unimportance
of the personal and political analogy. To him, as to the
mediaeval thinker, a particular application gave reality
and convincing proof of the philosophical generalization.
We are apt to forget how incident to poetic—to emotional
—conviction is this argument by particular analogy. We
dislike the political allegories and analogies in *The Faerie
Queene*, partly because we hold that great poetry should
not deal with historical particulars, and even more because
we half-consciously suspect Spenser of flattering the great
for his own advancement. But in fact, except in the
identification of Gloriana with Elizabeth and of Duessa
with Mary Queen of Scots, his historical allusions must
have been dangerous for himself. He makes a hero of
Lord Grey, when Lord Grey was under a cloud, and he
shows his devotion to Leicester after his death. The
references to the Queen of Scots in the person of Duessa
were resented by King James, though it is true that Elizabeth might be expected to appreciate them; but there is
no reason to suppose that Spenser wrote them to curry
favour. He was a zealous Protestant. If Mary survived
Elizabeth she would almost certainly be Queen of England,
and that might have meant the return of the times of her
bloody namesake. For a man of Spenser's views Mary
really was the incarnation of all that he hated in the Roman
Church. He hated her as a symbol of danger to all that
he loved in his country, as he worshipped Elizabeth as

the symbol of its safety and glory, and we must remember
that contemporaries could not know that Elizabeth would
die a natural death.

But even in this sense Elizabeth's identification with
Gloriana is relatively unimportant.   The Faerie Queene is
'Glory in my general intention,' the spiritual loveliness
which is the object of Prince Arthur's quest, and indis-
tinguishable from the Sapience of the Hymn to Heavenly
Love:

> 'Whose beautie filles the heavens with her light,
> And darkes the earth with shadow of her sight.'

In the four *Hymns* the poet was integrating the passion of
Holiness, and in that passion he included the human love
of man for woman, the divine love of God for man, and
the love of God and man alike for spiritual perfection.

That Spenser did regard earthly love as beautiful and
pure is proved by the fact that Amoret is twin-sister to
Belphoebe and, like her, immaculately conceived.   She is
the fosterling of Venus, and the Hymn to Venus, which
is sung by one of the lovers in the temple as Scudamour
makes his way to his bride, is significant as much of her
as of the goddess.   It is an interesting example of Spenser's
art: a free translation of Lucretius' great invocation, it is
crossed by memories of Chaucer's delightful picture in
the Prologue to *The Legend of Good Women*, of the birds'
love-making, as well as by a passage in the *Georgics*.   The
tone for a moment is playful, but the splendid rhythm
of the climax makes it clear that Spenser was serious in
his attempt to weave the philosophy of Lucretius into his
own.

Lucretius' Hymn opens his poem, and he attributes
to the goddess of Love the creation and direction of the
whole visible universe.   'Thou alone dost govern the
nature of things—without thee nothing comes forth into

the shining borders of light, nothing joyous and lovely is made' (Loeb translation). This becomes in Spenser:

> 'Thou art the root of all that joyous is
> Great God of man and women, Queen of th'ayre,
> Mother of laughter and welspringe of blisse.'
>
> (*F.Q.* IV. x. 47.)

It is improbable that Lucretius, any more than Spenser, thought of Venus as in reality a god. It appears to be fundamental in the thought of the Latin poet that the gods in no way interfere in the concerns of man. Lucretius is substituting a physical for a personal creative power. Spenser accepts the description of the physical impulse, but Lucretius' poetry creates for him as a sort of luminous shadow behind the physical 'a bringer of that joy.' He could not accept the merely material nature of beauty. He was fascinated and perturbed by its mystery, by the secret of its essence. It is not true, he finds, that beauty is merely a mixture of fair colours or of certain proportions:

> 'How vainly then do ydle wits invent
> That beauty is naught else, but mixture made
> Of colours faire, and goodly temp'rament,
> Of pure complexions, that shall quickly fade
> And passe away, like to a summer's shade,
> Or that it is but comely composition
> Or parts well measur'd with meet disposition.
>
> Hath white and red in it such wondrous powre
> That it can pierce through th' eyes into the heart?'
>
> (*H.B.* 64–72.)

There is, he seems to argue, something not contained in the separate physical elements which is needed to bring to birth our wonder and excitement. And the passion of love aroused by human beauty is more mysterious still:

'Why do not then the blossoms of the field,
Which are arrayed with much more orient hue,
And to the sense most daintie colours yield
Work like impression on the lookers' view?'

(*Ibid.*, 78–81.)

The passion excited is the reflection and proof of a divine
fire itself invisible, but like the disturbing influence in
space of an undiscovered planet. It is to this Queen of
th'ayre that his Hymn is directed. His Venus is born of
physical nature, but is nevertheless to Spenser of good
report, and she is at once the impulse to poetry and to
that upward striving ardour which is the essence of spiritual
life.

CHAPTER VI

'The Soul an impulse to herself'

An earlier chapter dealt with Spenser's poetry of the world of sense; but, beautiful as is that world, Spenser did not allow Sir Calidore to remain in it, and neither the poet himself nor his early readers like Milton regarded such poetry as his chief claim to immortality. To them he was a great philosophical and ethical poet: 'a better teacher than Scotus or Aquinas,' and it is clear that this was what he aspired to be. It is at least probable that Spenser himself and his great successor, so near him in time, understood the nature of his achievement better than the centuries which followed, uneasily conscious as they are that here is a great poet, but always questioning wherein that greatness lies.

Now the business of a philosophical poet is to unveil the mysteries of human experience in its heights and depths. Spenser, though he loved the world of sense, thought it almost accidental. It is 'not (his) wish nor prayer, but got by mere despair of wings.' The true life of man lies not in this temporal and material realm of mutability, but in the invisible world of mind. The soul's dealings with abstractions and values is the measure of its true character: the real tissue even of our secular exist-ence is not the visible world but our reactions to it. Our happiness, or unhappiness, for example, is something very lightly attached to external events, a fact of which the Elizabethans were intensely aware. Our life goes on be-hind the façade of our bodies and only the most general reference as a rule, or momentary revelations in times of crisis, passes our lips, or finds expression in our faces or in our actions. It is this inner life that is Spenser's Land of Faerie: it is with the greater movements in it that he must deal if he is to make good his claim to being a great ethical poet.

Professor Grierson in his *Cross Currents in English Literature of the Seventeenth Century* explicitly denies this claim for Spenser. He holds that 'the *Morte d'Arthur* and the *Orlando Furioso* are more impressive ethical poems than *The Faerie Queene*, because they are more human.' None of Spenser's characters, he asserts, 'assumes the proportions of Everyman face to face with one of the great elemental temptations or experiences of men.' It is my contention that a lack of sympathy with Spenser's method of expression has hidden from us his revelation of the great intimacies of life, and blinded us to his more profound thought. Critics have accepted as the dynamic centre of his teaching a particular form of Christianized Platonism supplemented by a superficial Aristotelian ethic, and when they failed to find any adequate expression of such doctrines, have found fault with the poet as inconsistent and trivial. Some inconsistencies due to the change of plan must be admitted, but they do not touch the main body of his great poetry.

Spenser differs from the nineteenth century in the anthropomorphic nature of his imagery; but he differs in another respect from his contemporary Shakespeare, and the fact that our study of Elizabethan literature tends to start from the dramatist, has been perhaps a greater hindrance to our understanding of *The Faerie Queene* than even our nineteenth-century preconceptions.

Spenser differs from Shakespeare in two ways. In the first place he gives direct expression to the spiritual quintessence of our experience—of the product in us of the mar-

riage of the 'external universe of things' and happenings
within our consciousness; while the dramatic poet necessarily gives the event and the external expression by word
or deed or look of the man's reaction to that event.   Lear
suffers the bereavement of Cordelia and dies of a broken
heart, and the physical oppression finds vent in the words
'Pray you, undo this button.'   His agony of mind has a
result on the material plane, and it is of that material
result he speaks.   We translate it back for ourselves into
the spiritual passion.

In the second place, Spenser generalizes, while Shakespeare particularizes.   Spenser deals with man's emotion
when the fact of decay or death, for example, is brought
home to him.   Lear is, no doubt, a terrific embodiment
of the tragedy of age, but our minds are to some extent
entangled in the details of his particular catastrophe.   The
wickedness of Goneril and Regan obscures their quality
as representatives of the inevitable and unconscious cruelty
of the advancing generation to its predecessor.   We forget
the anguish of bereavement as an ever-threatening element
in human life, in the realization that it is Cordelia who
lies dead before her time.   In Shakespeare's great tragedies
'quick-coming death' is itself 'a little thing' when we are
face to face with the deaths of Juliet, of Desdemona or of
Antony.   Spenser's medium, though naturally it loses
something, yet gains by its generalization.   When Everyman is most essentially human, it is the universality of
human ills that appals him, and that forces him out into
the abysses of existence.   And, ultimately, it is the poet's
office to bring us face to face with life itself, not with an
individual life.

The present tendencies of dramatic production suggest
a subconscious instinct that the dramatic form is inadequate.
Producers attempt to show by effects of lighting and by
symbolic staging the universal pattern on which the web

of a particular story is woven.   Again, modern criticism
seems to have proved two practices by which Shakespeare
escaped the limitations of his medium, and in so doing
recognized its inadequacy for the complete presentation
of his thought.   These are: his use of keywords and
images to suggest the theme of his play, and the freedom
with which he deals with time and space, manipulating
these tyrannic forces to his purpose.   It has been shown,
for example, that Shakespeare apparently gives us two
time-schemes in *Othello*.   In one, Desdemona is murdered
within a week of her arrival in Cyprus and scarcely more
of the marriage ceremony: in the other she and Othello
have had months, perhaps years, of perfect union before
the tragic misunderstanding.   The same sort of thing
occurs in *Lear*, while in *Antony and Cleopatra* time and
space become almost visible forces interacting with the
great *dramatis personae*.   These three plays were written
in the seventeenth century, but earlier, in *As you like it*,
the dramatist had laughingly suggested the relativity of
time to human emotion, and Hamlet knew that he could
be a king of infinite space in a nutshell, were it not for
his dreams.   The identification in the last plays of men
themselves with the stuff of dreams is but the inevitable
development of this, and Shakespeare at the end approxi-
mates to the thought of Spenser.   There is something of
the same distinction between narrative and dramatic poetry
on the one hand, and the poetry of the inner experience
which is Spenser's characteristic province on the other,
that Wordsworth drew between 'action' and 'suffering';
the one transitory and momentary, the other having the
nature of infinity.   The universalized emotion of Spenser's
'cloudy heaven' generated by no external action or event
partakes of this infinite quality.

But this does not mean that it is that inconceivable
being, man in the abstract, who is the hero and focus of

emotion in Spenser's poem. Inevitably it is the poet's
own inner experience, made available for the uses of
poetry by release from its relation to his external circumstances, which is the stuff of all the more vital parts.   We
can be sure that Spenser's personality is given in *The Faerie
Queene* as we can never be sure that Shakespeare's is in
any or all of his works.   From the more important figures,
from the stress laid on, and the recurrence of certain
incidents, we can build up a picture of his personality and
deduce the central moral problem, perhaps the central ethic
of his own life.

Wordsworth used the passage from *The Borderers* as a
motto to explain his purpose in *The White Doe of Rylstone*
—the purpose of showing that suffering 'obscure and dark'
is the human key to sublime existence.   It is probably
true that 'our sweetest songs are those that tell of saddest
thought,' not because pain is necessarily the fundamental
element of existence, but because it seems to be a condition of vivid consciousness in time.   On the other hand,
ecstasy of joy is a white radiance, in which the separate
colours of experience are lost.   Something similar is true
of the presentation of sin and virtue, and the idea that
Spenser's poetry has little to tell us of Everyman's intimate
and fundamental life is due in part to the misleading stress
on the virtues given by the titles of the books.   In the
poem itself the House of Alma is greatly inferior as poetry
to the dwelling of Mammon, the House of Holiness to
the Cave of Despair; and whenever the several knights
become true personifications of the virtues they represent,
the glamour is apt to fade, the allegory becomes obvious
and the morality trite.   On the other hand, the presentation of the temptations is subtle, manifold, opening out
vistas in the mysterious forest of human personality.   The
ethical doctrine negatively suggested in them is of a finer
quality than that of which there is positive expression.

As the present writer holds that the poem was originally written rather round the temptations than round the virtues, the final analysis of Spenser's message will deal chiefly with them.

It was suggested in the opening chapter that the sin of the first Book was what the mediaeval world called *accidie* or *acedia*.   Although the word occurs nowhere in Spenser, and is indeed very rare in Elizabethan literature, the moral disease appears to have been extremely prevalent at the time, and the allusions show that it had come to be considered 'the last infirmity of noble minds.'   *Accidie* is a profound distaste for life, resulting in deep melancholy and inertia and often leading to suicide.   Its analysis is the theme of Burton's *Anatomy of Melancholy* early in the next century.

This passion of melancholy, paralysing action and leading to the desire of death, is constantly appearing in Spenser's work.   The monkish form of *accidie* under the name of idleness leads the masque of the Seven Deadly Sins, who are Lucifera's councillors.   In the garden of Proserpine Spenser adds the temptation to sit on a silver stool, making it indeed the central point of the episode. Scudamour, who appears rather particularly to represent the poet, is, at his first introduction, a picture of despairing inertia.   Britomart finds him 'all wallowed upon the grassy ground' and raises him again and again, but each time he relapses into hopeless apathy:

> 'And downe again himself disdainfully
> Abjecting, th' earth with his faire forhead strooke:'

In fact, although it is in the first Book that the most complete presentation is given of the sin, it is the dominant temptation appearing in different circumstances and shapes throughout the original form of the poem.   As such it will be more convenient to take it last.

The temptations of Mammon or the world are presented
in three stages—the treasure chamber, the Hall of Ambition, and the garden of Proserpine. In all three—
particularly in the first and the third—the poet gives us,
not merely images of the baits to sin, but much more
pictures of the mental atmosphere in which the sinner is
entrapped. The first chamber represents the lure of
material wealth and of its symbol gold. It was with this
aspect that Milton identified Mammon, when he called
him 'the least erected spirit that fell' from Heaven. But
Spenser, although the sin had no real hold upon him, was
too much a son of the Renaissance to deny its value or to
be unaware of its attraction. By the use of shadows, of
dust and cobwebs and smoke, he at once enhances its
pictorial beauty and creates a world of mental squalid
splendour:

'That houses forme within was rude and strong,
    Lyke an huge cave hewne out of rocky clifte,
    From whose rough vaut the ragged breaches hong
    Embost with massy gold of glorious guifte,
    And with rich metall loaded every rifte,
    That heavy ruine they did seeme to threatt
    And over them Arachne high did lifte
    Her cunning web, and spred her subtile nett,
Enwrapped in fowle smoke and clouds more black then Jet.

Both roofe, and floore, and walls, were all of gold,
    But overgrowne with dust and old decay,
    And hid in darkenesse, that none could behold
    The hew thereof; for vew of cherefull day
    Did never in that house it selfe display,
    But a faint shadow of uncertein light:
    Such as a lamp, whose life does fade away,
    Or as the Moone, cloathed with clowdy night,
Does show to him that walkes in feare and sad affright.'

                    (*F.Q.* II. vii. 28, 29.)

The glare of the golden chamber is far more effective for the gloom which hangs over it, and the sin for which Mammon stands is linked to a world dark, grotesque and eerie, the centre of which is a terrified man touched fitfully by still moonlight.

The well-known passage in *Mother Hubberds Tale* on the 'Suters State' is like a gloss on the meaning of the court of Mammon's daughter. 'What hell it is,' cries Spenser, forgetting his story for a moment in the intensity of his own experience,

'in suing long to bide;

.   .   .   .   .

To fret thy soule with crosses and with cares;
To eate thy heart through comfortlesse dispaires;
To fawne, to crowche, to waite, to ride, to ronne,
To spend, to give, to want, to be undonne.'

'That curse,' he solemnly concludes, 'God send unto mine enemy.' The episode in *The Faerie Queene* has none of this intensity and it is here and here only that Guyon treats Mammon with courtesy, refusing gently the offer of his daughter's hand. It is probably an early piece of work: one feels that Spenser had not yet tasted the degradation of ambition, and the picture of Philotime and her suitors is like many in the mediaeval dream poems, little illuminated by Spenser's peculiar light.

The garden of Proserpine, on the other hand, has memories of a wealth of classical poetry as well as of Dante. Mammon leads Guyon

'Through griesly shadowes by a beaten path
Into a garden goodly garnished
With hearbs and fruits, whose kindes mote not be red.'
(*F.Q.* II. vii. 51.)

But which are

'Direful, deadly, blacke both leafe and bloome,
Fit to adorne the dead, and decke the drery tombe.'   (*Ibid.*)

There follows a list of the trees dark in colour and poisonous: and then enchanted, as it were, in this dark leafage 'in which she often used herself to shroud,' we catch a glimpse of the shadowy presence of Proserpine seated on a silver seat with the golden apple-tree of the Hesperides beside her.   The poet reminds us of all the stories in which the golden fruit has played a part, some of which are sunny enough, but the tree is here sinister, and its broad branches 'so fair and great that shadowed all the ground' stretch beyond the garden and dip themselves in the black river Cocytus that flows below the mound on which it stands.

Warton thought that the source of the passage was Claudian's *Rape of Proserpine*, but notes that Claudian makes Pluto woo his bride with promises of a garden whose flowers are as fair as any on earth.   Spenser needed a deeper note, and his garden of Proserpine is haunted by memories at once of the sad mediaeval Fairyland and of Dante's *Inferno*.   In the 'sad waves' of Cocytus, Pilate and Tantalus are both tormented.   The appeal to the eye is never forgotten, but the details—the endless spreading trees, shadowing the ground and partly hiding the sinister river, the evil gleam of the golden apples, and above all, the thick arbour with its silver seat, which is the moral centre of the picture, and seems to be Spenser's own invention—all these conjure up the atmosphere of the valley of the shadow of spiritual death, of a world in which there is no sun or air of invigorating spiritual aspiration. In the first two chambers the evil of the desire of worldly wealth and power is exhibited, in the third the burden of its possession.   The heavy weight on a mind so pre-occupied is suggested with infinite subtlety, and the essence of the sin is seen to be its paralysing effect on the soul. Guyon refuses to seat himself, but he escapes barely with his life, so that when he returns to living light,

> 'All so soon as his enfeebled spright
>   Gan sucke this vitall aire into his brest,
>   As overcome with too exceeding might
>   The life did flit away out of her nest,
> And all his senses were with deadly fit opprest.'   (*F.Q.* II. vii. 66.)

In this swoon he continues a long time and were it not for a guardian angel and afterwards Prince Arthur he would have been slain.   The garden of Proserpine is the true evil counterpart to the garden of Adonis; the garden of death is set over against the garden of life.

Contrary to the apparently common opinion, the crude temptation of the flesh as represented in the Bower of Bliss was without allure for Spenser.   This is shown by his significant alterations in the text of the *Jerusalem Delivered*. In Tasso the lover and victim of the Enchantress Armida is the hero of this part of the poem: in Spenser the lover is a young man, who is barely introduced and for this episode only, while the hero of the book watches Acrasia's wiles apparently quite unmoved and then rushes out and binds her.   Milton's reference to the sin in *Paradise Lost* shows the same attitude, and he probably recognized in this too his affinity with Spenser.   The later poem owes much to Guyon's adventures—supplemented by Giles Fletcher's imitation in *Christ's Victory on Earth*—but the temptations of Acrasia are explicitly rejected as unable to affect any of the greater sons of men.   In the infernal council held to consider how the Messiah may be corrupted, Belial advises thus:

> 'Set women in his eye and in his walk
>   Among daughters of men the fairest found.'

But Satan returns 'quick answer':

> 'Belial, in much uneven scale thou weigh'st
>   All others by thyself . . .
>   . . . Among the sons of men

How many have with a smile made small account
Of beauty and her lures . . .
                                    on worthier things intent.
He whom we attempt is wiser far
Than Solomon, of more exalted mind,
How would one look from his majestic brow
Seated as on the top of Virtue's hill
Discountenance her despised.'

                                    (*P.R.* Bk. II. ll. 153 ff.)

Spenser, too, 'easily shunned' such temptations: the Bower
of Bliss is a beautiful example of his style in writing, but
it. is an excrescence on the aesthetic and moral plan of the
poem.

But one temptation in *Paradise Regained* appears to
include a memory of Acrasia's Bower.   The great description of the banquet in the desert seems to owe something
to the *Song of the Rose*.   That song is translated very nearly
word for word from Tasso, but Spenser has increased its
languorous cadence by lengthening the line.   The quintessence of the temptation for Spenser is the feeling of futility
of moral effort which comes with realization of the transience
of loveliness. 'Let us eat and drink for to-morrow we die.'
And yet mortality, the thought of 'ladies dead and lovely
knights' is the final grace of such beauty.

'So passeth in the passing of a day
    Of mortal life, the leafe, the bud, the flowre,
    Ne more doth flourish after first decay,
    That earst was sought to decke both bed and bowre,
    Of many a Ladie, and many a Paramowre:
    Gather therefore the Rose, whilst yet is prime,
    For soone comes age, that will her pride deflowre.'

                                    (*F.Q.* II. xii. 75.)

So Milton, though he had refused to present the more
direct appeal, yet makes his banquet a symbol of subtly
sweet beauty and the sad enchantment

'Of faery damsels met in forest wide
By knights of Logres or of Lyones,
Lancelot, or Pelleas or Pellenore.'   (*P.R.* II. 359.)

The subject of Book IV, I suppose to have been Wrath
originally, though examples of that sin are scattered through
the last three books, and as suggested above, the Pyrochles
of Book II appears to belong here.   The subject of canto
viii is always, particularly in the four earlier books, significant, and here the second and more important episode of
that canto is the overthrow by Prince Arthur of the giant
Corflambo, who as the poem stands is probably a personification of savage lust, but shows signs of having been at
first intended as an embodiment of the tyrannical cruelty
of the East.   We first see him

'Ryding upon a Dromedare on hie,
Of stature huge, and horrible of hew,
That would have mar'd a man his dreadfull face to vew.

For from his fearefull eyes two fierie beames,
More sharpe then points of needles did proceede,
Shooting forth farre away two flaming streames,
Full of sad powre, that poysonous bale did breede,
To all, that on him lookt without good heed,
And secretly his enemies did slay:
Like as the Basiliske of serpents seede,
From powrefull eyes close venim doth convay
Into the lookers hart, and killeth farre away.'
                          (*F.Q.* IV. viii. 38, 39.)

The rescued squire explains that the giant

'by his strength rule to himselfe did gaine
Of many nations into thraldome led
And mighty kingdomes of his force adred.'   (*Ibid.*, 47.)

Whatever the vice for which Corflambo stands, the image
itself shows Spenser's hatred of the attributes of the ruthless
conqueror.

The ferocity of Lord Grey's policy in Ireland, which Spenser upholds both in the fifth Book of *The Faerie Queene* and in the *View of the state of Ireland*, has suggested to some readers that the poet was himself harsh and cruel and admired such ruthless conquerors.   It is true that he has, on the one hand, little or no sympathy with those of humble station, who are generally called 'the rabble rout.'   Artegall, after the death of the communistic giant, hesitates to put his followers to death, not from mercy, but because he was loth

'his noble hands t'embrue
In the base blood of such a rascall crew.'

(*F.Q.* V. ii. 52.)

On the other hand, Prince Arthur is throughout and particularly in the earlier books always on the side of the oppressed, and the Red-Crosse knight is represented, in the preface, as being a 'clownish' young man.   The truth is that the allegorizing habit had dyed the poet's mind so deeply, that he does not distinguish between the sinner and the sin which he wishes to scourge out of existence. The rout that supports the communistic giant or attacks the House of Alma are undoubtedly made alive by traits which Spenser has borrowed from his knowledge of the Irish kerns, but on the other hand he identifies the kerns with abstract evil qualities, as the seventeenth-century Puritans identified their religious and political opponents with the Philistines, whom the Israelites conceived themselves divinely commanded to exterminate.   The Irish were to Spenser the enemies of order, culture and harmony; for 'they do use all the beastly behaviour that may be to oppress all men; they spoyle as well the subject as the enemy; they steale, they are cruell and bloudye, full of revenge and delighting in deadly execution, licentious, swearers and blasphemers, common ravishers of women and murtherers of children.'   The charges are no doubt

true: the Irish had been reduced to the state of savages
by centuries of ill-treatment.   Spenser saw the result, and
he took that result as symbolic of the reign of Satan upon
earth.   His censure of the Bardic song, which he epitomizes
in the *View* shows how far he was from the brutal ideals of
Marlowe.   The song celebrates, he says, 'a most notorious
thief and wicked outlaw' and praises him 'that he was none
of those idell milk-sops that was brought up by the fire-side,
but that most of his dayes he spent in crimes and valyaunt
enterprises; that he did never eate his meate before he had
wonne it with his sworde; that he was not slugging all
night in a cabin under his mantell, but used comonly
to keepe others waking to defend theyr lives, and did
light his candell at the flames of theyr howses to leade
him in the darkness; that the day was his night and the
night his day; that he loved not to lye long wooing of
wenches to yield unto him, but where he came he tooke
by force the spoyle of other mens love, and left but lamentations to their lovers; that his music was not the harpe,
nor layes of love, but the cryes of people, and clanking of
armour; and that finally, he died, not bewayled of many,
but made many wayle when he died, that dearly bought
his death.'   This might well be a description of a hero of
Marlowe.   Spenser may have admired the energy of this
ideal, but he hates violence and the doctrine that might
is right.   His ideal man is poles apart from Tamburlaine.

For Spenser the chief temptation had always seemed
to be to *accidio*, to succumb to that deep, passionate lethargy
which lay in wait for so many in his own day, and which
in some form is indeed the chief enemy of spiritual achievement.   The greatest Elizabethan treatment of the disease
is, as I have said, in *Hamlet*, but the significance of Shakespeare's treatment has been partly overlooked, because we
regard Hamlet's melancholy as the result of particular
causes—however much critics may disagree on the nature

of the particular cause.   The central poetic fact of *Hamlet*
is the hero's profound distaste for life, not what has brought
that distaste about.   Shakespeare builds up reasons for
the melancholy, because without some external excitements
the distemper would appear either pathological or senti-
mental.   He piles up the moral shocks to which his hero
is subjected—his mother's early second marriage, his
father's murder, his friends' treachery, Ophelia's apparent
time-serving, even the loss of a kingdom—but it is quite
needless to ask which has been most potent to produce his
state of mind, so long as we are convinced that circumstances make it inevitable that a noble nature should have
fallen into that abyss.   From this point of view Hamlet's
'mystery' and the Red-Crosse knight's encounter with
Despair are close parallels.

It is worth while to place beside Spenser's passage two
key speeches of Hamlet—the one to Rosencrantz and
Guildenstern in which he sees 'the majestical world' a
'foul and pestilent congregation of vapours'; and the
soliloquy which has always been regarded as the central
passage in the play: 'To be or not to be; that is the question.'   The burden of his words to the men he still holds
for friends, is that nothing can delight him.   He 'sees
not feels' the radiance of the universe, the divinity of
mankind; and the spring of action is broken.   The prose
form indicates that the rhythmic beat of life has stopped.

In the soliloquy a creature caught in what he feels to
be the horrible trap of existence utters his despair:

> 'For who would bear the whips and scorns of time,
> The oppressor's wrong, the proud man's contumely
> The pangs of despised love, the law's delay,
> The insolence of office, and the spurns
> That patient merit of the unworthy takes
> When he himself might his quietus make
> With a bare bodkin?   Who would fardels bear

To grunt and sweat under a weary life
But that the dread of something after death
. . . puzzles the will
And makes us rather bear those ills we have
Than fly to others that we know not of?'

The evils named are quite obviously *not* Hamlet's peculiar burdens: the poet has in fact almost forgotten his hero and is, like Spenser before him, gripped by the ultimate question of the value of existence—'To be or not to be.' Hamlet is overwhelmed by an intense distaste for life as most men—as the poet himself—have to live it, and this despair brings with it the impulse to self-slaughter.

For Hamlet melancholy is a deadly chill, which paralyses action and annihilates all joy in beauty. To Spenser too, it is the enemy of the creative force in life, and when Una's marriage to the Red-Crosse knight brings virtue to earth

'all the time sweet music did apply
Her curious skill, the warbling notes to play
To drive away the dull melancholy.'   (*F.Q.* I. xii. 38.)

But for Spenser as for the Red-Crosse knight this melancholy has the attractive force of gravity. When the Red-Crosse comes into the presence of Despair it is 'as he were charmed with enchaunted rimes.' The young man Trevisan, who has barely escaped with his life from Despair, tells Red-Crosse

'His subtill tongue, like dropping hony mealt'th
Into the hart, and searcheth every vaine,
That ere one be aware by secret stealth
His powre is reft, and weaknesse doth remaine.'   (*F.Q.* I. ix. 31.)

Hamlet is afraid of death: he is brought to a standstill, since death itself may be no refuge; but for Spenser, as for the Oriental mind, death had always an intense fascination. E. K., in a gloss on a passage in the October Eclogue of *The Shepheards Calender*, quotes from a lost poem of

Spenser the line 'the deep delight that is in death.' The
feeling is apparently not uncommon in a certain type of
mind. James, in his *Varieties of Religious Experience*, gives
several illustrations, which perhaps suggest that it is rather
peculiarly incident to the creative imagination. A notable
example is a passage from Tolstoi's autobiography which
describes his despair and impulse towards suicide preceding the crisis of conversion. 'It cannot be said exactly,'
Tolstoi writes, 'that I wished to kill myself, for the force
which drew me away from life was fuller, more powerful,
more general than any mere desire. It was a force like
my old aspiration to live, only it compelled me in the
opposite direction. It was an aspiration of my whole
being to get out of life.' This might be a prose translation
of the effect of Despair on Trevisan and the Red-Crosse
knight.

The dwelling of Despair is set in landscape that in two
or three lines gives the quintessence of Browning's *Childe
Roland*. It is a cave whose natural fearfulness—

> 'Dark, dolefull, drerie, like a greedie grave
> That still for carrion carcases doth crave'—

is made to seem poisonous by the blighted trees around it:

> 'old stocks and sticks of trees
> Whereon nor fruit, nor leafe was ever seen.'

The figure of Despair himself suggests the repulsiveness of
social outcasts, but his majestic voice sounds all the stops
in the organ of tragedy. There is first the insinuation of
remorse or intolerable self-hatred, 'he should die, who
merits not to live' (We remember Hamlet's words, 'I could
accuse me of such things that it were better my mother
had not borne me'). But he quickly passes from that to
the great verses that seem to lay the whole burden of
human weariness upon our shoulders. The Red-Crosse

knight had tried to rescue one of Despair's victims and
Despair reproaches him:

> 'Who travels by the wearie wandring way
> To come unto his wished home in haste
> And meetes a flood, that doth his passage stay,
> Is not great grace to helpe him over past?
> Why wilt not let him passe that long hath stood
> Upon the bancke, yet wilt thyselfe not passe the flood.
>
> He there does now enjoy eternall rest
> And happie ease, which thou dost want and crave
> And further from it daily wanderest;
> What if some little paine the passage have
> That makes frail flesh to feare the bitter wave,
> Is not short pain well borne, that brings long ease
> And lays the soul to sleep in quiet grave?
> Sleep after toile, port after stormie seas,
> Ease after warre, death after life does greatly please.'

(F.Q. I. ix. 39, 40.)

The knight replies with an image that invokes a spirit of
noble discipline to repel the insidious charm:

> 'The soldier may not move from watchful sted
> Nor leave his stand, untill his Captain bed.' *(Ibid.,* 41.)

But the invigorating thought is lost in Despair's vision
of an Epicurean universe wherein helpless atoms rise and
fall continually, without responsibility, without result. The
useless vigil is over, says Despair

> 'And he that points the centonell his roome
> Doth licence him depart at sound of morning droome.'

Moreover, we are all helpless in the hands of the Ruler
of the universe:

> 'Is not his deed what ever thing is done
> In heaven or earth?   Did not he all create
> To die againe? all ends that was begonne.
> Who then can strive with strong necessitie
> That holds the world in his still chaunging state?' *(Ibid.,* 42.)

But though we are helpless, we shall be held responsible and right and wrong are utterly confused:

'The longer life, I wote the greater sin,
  The greater sin, the greater punishment.
  All those great battels, which thou boasts to win,
  Through strife, and bloodshed, and avengement,
  Now praysed, hereafter deare thou shalt repent.
  For life must life, and bloud must bloud repay.
  Is not enough thy evil life forespent?
  For he that once hath missed the right way
The further he doth goe, the further he doth stray.

  Then do no further goe, no further stray,
  But here lie downe and to thy rest betake.'   (*Ibid.*, 43, 44.)

and gathering up all the ills of human life:

'Fear, sickness, age, loss, labour, sorrow, strife,
  Pain, hunger, cold'

he cries out passionately:

'Death is the end of woes; die soon O Faeries sonne.'   (*Ibid.*, 47.)

Hamlet is brought to the verge of suicide by the particular circumstances of his life, though as we have seen—whether by inadvertence on the part of the poet or of intent—once he has reached the centre of the dark cloud, his despair reaches out and draws in the miseries of human life in general. The Red-Crosse knight's adventure expresses the same spiritual agony—perhaps more subtly untrammelled by particular details. We have a faint distaste for critics who see in Hamlet a reflection of their own problems and inner life, but Everyman is intended by the poet to see himself in the Red-Crosse knight.

To Spenser this was the fundamental temptation—the refusal of effort, the rejection of life. Santayana has said that Protestantism mistakes vitality for the spiritual life.

If it is a mistake, Spenser came very near to making it, but by vitality is not meant merely physical vigour. He did give a high value to physical exhilaration because he believed it stimulated the spiritual ardour. Prince Arthur's vision of the Faerie Queene comes at the climax of simple natural enjoyment, when 'life touch(es) lips with immortality.' Prince Arthur describes how

> 'Raunging the forest wide on courser free
> The fields, the floods, the heavens with one consent
> Did seem to laugh on me and forward mine intent'
>
> *(F.Q.* I. ix. 12.)

and after the rapture so induced the Faerie Queene appears. The music that Colin Clout played to the dancing lily maidens is, as it were, the fragrance of this vital joy, and is in itself a charm against the great sin of *accidie*, of turning away from life. But Spenser aspired to sing of the pure joyous activity of soul when the life of sense has been laid asleep. For him, as for Wordsworth, the main ethical problem was how to deal with the inevitable passing of youth's creative joy. In the *Leech-Gatherer* Wordsworth tells how 'We poets in our youth begin in gladness, But thereof cometh in the end despondency and madness.' The 'gladness' described at the beginning of the poem is of the same quality as Prince Arthur's delight in the passage just quoted. In Wordsworth's case this mood soon passes and

> 'As high as (he has) mounted in delight
> In his dejection (does he) sink as low,'

and then comes the vision-like appearance of the Leech-Gatherer, at once linked with the torpid earth by the immobility of his 'extreme old age' and with the sublimity of our mortal nature by his fortitude in bearing 'the more than human weight' of his misfortunes. Wordsworth offers us this god-like fortitude as consolation for the lost radiance of youth, but his presentation of it is hesitating and momentary, and the consolation itself is chill and grey.   Spenser had always believed that physical beauty and the delight it inspires is but a shadow of that spiritual experience to which he gives the name of Sapience,

> 'Whose beautie filles the heavens with her light,
> And darkes the earth with shadow of her sight
>
> .   .   .   .   .
>
> In which (men) see such admirable things
> As carries them into an extasy'
>
> (*H.H.B.* 228–9, 260–1.)

so that they

> 'All happie joy and full contentment fynd.'
>
> (*Ibid.*, 287.)

The amazing quality of the poetry in the Despair passage seems to assure us of his power to tell of

> 'that immortall fire
> Which learned minds enflameth with desire.'

For the quality of the Despair passage lies in this, that while the whole scene is hideous and intentionally hideous and repellent, yet the general effect is overwhelmingly beautiful.   Spenser has here solved the problem of distilling strange abstract beauty without any beautiful image.   Nowhere, perhaps, is the magical power of poetry to conjure up that ethereal essence so perfectly illustrated.   It is, as it were, a vision hanging in the sky, created from the reflected radiance of the furnaces of sorrow.   But it is a negative vision, and in the final book the poet tremblingly hoped to be made the prophet of the perfect light:

> 'Ah! whither dost thou now thou greater Muse
> Me from these woods and pleasing forests bring?
> And my frail spirit (that doth oft refuse
> This too high flight, unfit for her weake wing)
> Lift up aloft to tell of Heavens King.'

Had he lived to complete the last canto of the Book of Mutabilitie, he would have told us of his vision of the eternal world which subsists behind this physical one that we perceive by the senses, the world in which the armies of the living God rest in creative activity. That seems to be the meaning of the last line of *The Faerie Queene*:

'O that great Sabaoth God, graunt me that Sabbaths sight.'

Appendix

Since most authorities believe that Bryskett is recording an historical occasion in his *Introduction of Giraldi's Discourses*, and since the latest writers put that occasion early in 1582, some discussion of Bryskett's book is needed. For Bryskett represents Spenser as refusing to give an account of ethical philosophy because 'I have already undertaken a work tending to the same effect, which is in *heroical verse*, under the title of a *Faerie Queene*, to represent all the Morall virtues, assigning to every virtue a knight to be the patron and defender of the same; in whose actions and feats of arms and chivalry, the operations of that virtue, whereof he is to be the protector, are to be expressed, and the vices and unruly appetites that oppose themselves against the same, to be beaten downe and overcome.' If then Bryskett is reporting Spenser accurately we must admit that by the date of the conversation Spenser had already reconstructed his scheme, although it does not necessarily follow that it had been worked out or the new passages written. It is noticeable that Prince Arthur is not mentioned.

This speech of the poet has been quoted in nearly every account of *The Faerie Queene*, but Bryskett's book itself is not easily accessible and therefore serious discussion of its value as an authority has been hampered. It has never been reprinted, and copies of the original are comparatively scarce. The Bodleian Library has one, the British Museum two, and America two, but Cambridge University Library, for example, has none. The intrinsic value is perhaps slight, but even apart from its connection with Spenser the light which it throws on the manner of thought of the Elizabethans is considerable. Bryskett follows the original, so far as the philosophical argument is concerned, fairly closely, differing from it chiefly by omission; but in one place where the twelve moral virtues are described, he patches the text from another Italian writer Piccolomini, because he considers his main authority inadequate. Thus his selection of Giraldi as giving a satisfactory reconstruction of what 'the Greeks and Romans

139

have confusedly left written' and his modifications of Giraldi himself afford a fairly clear personal statement. A reprint would be useful.

Bryskett's book was not published till 1606, but the body of it purports to have been written before the death in 1593 of Lord Grey de Wilton to whom it is addressed. It is dedicated, however, to Robert Cecil, to whom Bryskett expresses himself deeply obliged for his part in obtaining his release from prison in Flanders in 1602.

The introduction records how Bryskett is visited at his cottage near Dublin by eight distinguished friends, who find him with Martin Smith his apothecary. Smith thinks that Bryskett needs to be purged of the melancholy humour which has led him to resign a useful and honourable post and to retire to this solitary spot. Others of the party agree with the apothecary and Bryskett is led to defend his action on the ground that he has retired in order to engage in philosophical studies, the most important occupation a man can have. He laments that he is hampered by his ignorance of the classical tongues and tries to induce Spenser, who, he says, is both perfect in the languages and learned in philosophy, to deliver there and then a philosophical lecture. Spenser softens his own refusal by suggesting that Bryskett might read to the company his translation of Giraldi's *Discourses*, remarking that he will thereby show that his leisure has been put to profitable use. Bryskett points out that his translation is not in its final state and the company feel that the complete translation would take too long. So it is arranged that he is to give a free version of the argument having his papers at hand to consult. He explains that even in its shortened form his matter will occupy many hours, and his guests agree to return on the two following days.

Giraldi's *Discourses* also took three days to deliver, but not only are the speakers other than those of Bryskett, but the setting is of an entirely different character. Bryskett's are all historical persons who spent the greater part of their active lives in Ireland. The philosophical theory in Giraldi was laid down by one Lelio, and Bryskett himself takes his part, the exactness of the correspondence with the original being accounted for by his use of his rough translation. But the questions, objections and comments of Lelio's friends are assigned by Bryskett to the different members of his own party, and for the closeness of those speeches to the original no explanation is attempted. No single figure in Giraldi is represented throughout by the same person in Bryskett's book, but an attempt appears to have been made to assign to his friends the sort of thing they might have said. Thus John Long, Primate of Armagh, takes a leading part, usually that given to 'Torquato' in the original; but nearly all comments which indicate something like first-hand knowledge of classical writers are spoken by him, whosoever the speaker in the original may be. Again, one of the soldiers is particularly interested in the question of the morality of the duel.

After the introduction, which has no connection with Giraldi, Spenser is silent till the third dialogue. Then he speaks six times, taking the place of Torquato in the original, and five of these six speeches occur in the nine last pages of the book. These five are all concerned with the question of the immortality of the 'understanding.' Finally Spenser says 'doth your author meane . . . that there are in us two several soules, the one sensitive and morall, and the other intellective and divine?' To this Bryskett replies: 'Nothing less . . . for that were manifest heresie as well in Philosophie as in Christianity.' Having in view that the Primate has taken up to this stage all the characteristically intelligent comments of Torquato, the explanation of Spenser's intrusion here is probably the heretical quality of the passages.[1]

Mr. Plomer and Mr. Cross in their useful monograph on Bryskett [2] assign 1582 as the date of the first conversation, though they admit that the third day's meeting cannot have taken place till 1585, and the text makes the three days consecutive. The argument in favour of the date 1582 is that the discussion turns on Bryskett's resignation of his post of Clerk to the Council, which they think must, therefore, have been very recent. Now a letter from Bryskett to Walsingham, dated 10th May, 1582, records with joy his long-delayed release from office and prays the minister's countenance for his successor. But it is quite clear in the letter that the release is very recent indeed, while both Bryskett's words to Lord Grey and Spenser's to Bryskett in the discussion imply that his translation of Giraldi is the fruit of the leisure which Grey had procured for him by allowing him to resign. Some time, then, must have elapsed before the first discussion.

On the other hand, the evidence that the third day's conversation was not before 1585 is conclusive. For the dialogue brings out that

[1] But it might be argued that Spenser held views not dissimilar.

[2] H. R. Plomer and T. P. Cross, *The Life and Correspondence of Lodowick Bryskett*. Chicago, 1927.

Lord Grey de Wilton has been succeeded in his office of Lord Deputy by Sir John Perrot, and that the latter has had some opportunity to show his policy. Bryskett represents himself as praising 'the wisdome, valour and foresight of our Lord Deputie.' To this Sir Robert Dillon responds that 'the course holden by our present Lord Deputie, doth promise us a continuance, if not a bettering, of this our peace and quietnesse. My Lord Grey hath plowed and harrowed the rough ground to his hand.' Now Grey's successor as Lord Deputy reached Ireland in June, 1584, and as the Dialogues are supposed to take place in spring the date may be assumed to be early in 1585. If then the circumstances are historically accurate this must have been the date of the meeting; although if Bryskett may be supposed to have deviated from historical accuracy merely by making the discussions take place on consecutive days, when in fact they were scattered over some years, 1583 seems a rather more natural time for the original discussion.

But, in fact, a closer examination of the book confirms the impression that if there ever were such a meeting, its circumstances have been considerably modified to suit a literary conception. The greatest of all these Renaissance dialogues was Castiglione's *Courtier* and his admiration for that model is the key, I believe, to much in Bryskett's setting. For example, it shakes one's confidence in the view that the book must have been completely written by 1593, because although it is dedicated to Salisbury the main body is addressed to Lord Grey de Wilton, who died in that year, when one finds that the *Courtier* is addressed to 'Maister Alfonsus Ariosto' but dedicated to Michael de Sylva, Bishop of Viseo, because Ariosto is dead. Two ladies and ten men take part in the discussions in the *Courtier*. Bryskett has no ladies, but there are ten men of the party on the first day, though Smith the apothecary drops out after that. The inclusion, however, of a man of Smith's condition in a gathering of people of considerable importance is perhaps significant. He may have been brought in to produce the number ten.

Such a parallel might be considered far-fetched were it not for a rather curious fact. In what Hoby calls the 'Proheme' to the fourth book, Castiglione laments that three of those who took part in the discussions were dead by the time he wrote his account. The historical setting of the discussion dates it in 1507 and Castiglione in his epistle to de Sylva says that he made the first sketch shortly after the death of the Duke of Urbino, which took place in 1508, 'whyle the savour of the virtues of Duke Guidubaldo was fresh in my mynde'; 'the which I accomplished,' he goes on to say, 'in a few dayes, myndinge in time to amends those faults that spronge of the desire that I had speedilie to paye this debt. But fortune now manie yeares hath alwayes kept me under in such continuall travayles, that I could never get leyser to bringe it to the passe that my feeble judgement might be throughlie satisfied withall.' The book was not published till 1528, twenty-one years after the discussion was supposed to take place. By the time the Epistle was written the Duchess, the centre of Castiglione's circle, and three more of the interlocutors were dead. The epistle, indeed, is a beautiful lament for the glory of those past days. The author takes up his old manuscript 'and suddenlie, at the first blush by reason of the title, I tooke no little grief, which in proceedinge forward increased much more, rememberinge that the greater part of them that are brought in to reason, are now dead.'

Now Bryskett's book was published in 1606, and he takes, as we saw above, considerable trouble in the third dialogue to give the date of that meeting as being 1585—that is twenty-one years before. Moreover, as in the *Courtier*, most if not all of those who took part in the discussion, with the exception of Bryskett himself, are dead. Long, Primate of Armagh, died in 1589; Captain Carleill in 1593; Sir Robert Dillon and probably Captain Norreis in 1597. There are two Warham St. Legers, and the elder died in 1597 and the younger in 1600. Spenser died in 1599, and Dawtrey in 1601. 'Mr. Dormer, the Queen's solicitor,' does not appear in the *D.N.B.*, but the number of the dead, even without him, exceeds those in Castiglione's book. In both cases we have at least seven voices from the past, the man for whom the book was written and at least six more. I should expect Mr. Dormer to have died early, for he takes a considerable part in the discussion, and it is noticeable that on the whole—apart from Bryskett—the chief speakers are those who have been longest dead. The Primate dying first has most assigned to him, while Warham St. Leger who is almost certainly the younger, who died in 1600, takes no part in the discussion at all. Dawtrey was the last to die, and his part may have been written in his lifetime, but it is noticeable that he is the comic figure of the party. It has been suggested by a descendant that he was the original of Sir

John Falstaff, and Bryskett's treatment of him certainly lends support to this view. Bryskett as host had warned the party that he could only offer them food meet for philosophers, and Dawtrey exclaims with a consternation which makes the others laugh, 'yet let not our dinner, I pray you, be so temperate for Sir Robert Dillon's words, but that we may have a cup of wine, for the Scripture telleth us that wine gladdeth the heart of man.'

Now Spenser dies later than any except St. Leger and Dawtrey, and I suspect that his part was added after the others, possibly as late as 1604 when there was a proposal to issue a folio edition of *The Faerie Queene*. It was twice entered in the Stationer's Register in that year, although it was not published till 1609. We saw above that he never intervenes in the philosophical argument until at the very end he is used to voice 'obstinate questionings' which Bryskett denounces as heretical, and it is easy to see how even the famous passage in the introduction may be an insertion. For the production of the translation of Giraldi follows naturally on Bryskett's defence of his philosophical leisure, and his lament for the absence in English of summaries of the classics such as existed in Italian.

It is, then, possible that this account of the plan of *The Faerie Queene* was written long after the *Prefatory Letter* was in Bryskett's hands. He must have read his book over when preparing it for the press and adding the dedication to Salisbury. Even had Spenser originally given a description of his poem, in the twenty years that had elapsed Bryskett's memory might well be confused. On the other hand, if the occasion was historical and Bryskett reproduces substantially what Spenser said, according to the theory here advanced, the eight books might well be in their present form by 1585, while the scheme, as amended after Harvey's strictures was probably in existence by 1582. Bryskett's book is, therefore, negligible in the present connection.